TOMMY VICKNAIR
SPENCE STEPHENS

One
IN THE LORD

You 2 Can Have a Great Marriage!

TATE PUBLISHING
AND ENTERPRISES, LLC

One in the Lord
Copyright © 2011 by Tommy Vicknair & Spence Stephens. All rights reserved.

No part of this publication may be reproduced, stored in a retrieval system or transmitted in any way by any means, electronic, mechanical, photocopy, recording or otherwise without the prior permission of the author except as provided by USA copyright law.

This book is designed to provide accurate and authoritative information with regard to the subject matter covered. This information is given with the understanding that neither the author nor Tate Publishing, LLC is engaged in rendering legal, professional advice. Since the details of your situation are fact dependent, you should additionally seek the services of a competent professional.

The opinions expressed by the author are not necessarily those of Tate Publishing, LLC.

Published by Tate Publishing & Enterprises, LLC
127 E. Trade Center Terrace | Mustang, Oklahoma 73064 USA
1.888.361.9473 | www.tatepublishing.com

Tate Publishing is committed to excellence in the publishing industry. The company reflects the philosophy established by the founders, based on Psalm 68:11,
"The Lord gave the word and great was the company of those who published it."

Book design copyright © 2011 by Tate Publishing, LLC. All rights reserved.
Cover design by Kellie Vincent
Interior design by Sarah Kirchen

Published in the United States of America

ISBN: 978-1-61346-431-1
1. Religion / Christian Life / Love & Marriage
2. Religion / Christian Life / Personal Growth
11.09.7

Mother Teresa said that "Love is repaid by love alone!" ... To all my family and loved ones, colleagues, heroes, and to Tom, for their insights and everything inspirational that went into crafting this book. Your love is alive in these pages. With hope, gratitude, and respect,

—Spence

To God, for loving me first. To my wonderful wife, Elaine, for her love and for not giving up on me.

To all the people God has put in my path to help me learn to love and forgive. To Spence, for his partnership in writing this book.

—Tommy

TABLE OF CONTENTS

INTRODUCTION

    A Christ-Centered Marriage........................... 11

    An Overview of the Chapters......................... 13

    FINDING A WILLINGNESS TO CHANGE

    A Journey in Faith 17

    And They Lived Happily Ever After? 19

    But I'm Happy!...................................... 22

    Sinking in Reality................................... 26

    A Moment of Revelation 28

    Priorities: Put God First in Your Life.................. 29

    God's Intervention: Love Your Enemies 30

A PERSONAL TRANSFORMATION

    Being Open to Change 35

    Sharing Christ with Others 37

    Choosing the Right Path in Life 42

    Lord, Change Me................................... 44

SHARING THE FRUIT OF THE SPIRIT

The Spirit Versus the Flesh 49

Who's in Control? 55

Instant Feedback 57

The Long-Term Effects 59

THE TWO SHALL BECOME ONE

A Spiritual Union 61

Love One Another 64

So Why Isn't Everyone Having a Great Marriage? 66

    Addictions and Distractions 68

    "Judgmentalism" 71

    Resistance to Change 72

    Loss of Faith in Marriage 75

Living in the Holy Spirit 76

LIVING A BALANCED LIFE

The FISHES Assessment 79

The FISHES Questionnaire 81

    Family 82

    Intellect 85

    Social Life 85

    Health 89

    Economics 92

    Spirituality 94

Balance and Connection between FISHES Areas 96

A BLUEPRINT FOR MARRIAGE

- Success Mapping 99
- The Basic Requirements of Wives and Husbands 101
  - A Wife's Basic Requirements 102
  - A Husband's Basic Requirements............... 108
  - Living a Christian Marriage 113

DEALING WITH LIFE'S DIFFICULTIES

- Making Time for Each Other........................119
- Managing Conflicts 125
- Constructively Communicating..................... 129
- Taking Responsibility for Negative Emotions 133
- Practicing Forgiveness 134
- Working Together 136

A GREAT MARRIAGE IS LIFE CHANGING

- Bringing Home the Joy............................141
- Relationships 101: Marriage As a Model for All Relationships 152
- The Spiritual Steps to a Great Marriage............... 156
- Unconditional Love as Spiritual Inspiration 162

INTRODUCTION

A CHRIST-CENTERED MARRIAGE

God took a marriage on the brink of failure—my own—and transformed it into a great marriage. My wife and I have been happily married over thirty-nine years. This past year we celebrated our forty-seven anniversary.

Over the course of this book, I will share with you the ups, the downs, the mistakes we made in those early years. I'll then share how we altered the path our lives and relationship would take by focusing upon the life and teachings of Christ as our guide. With Him at the center of our lives and marriage, a transformation began to happen and the fruit of the Spirit blossomed into wonderful new and enriched blessings of forgiveness, love, joy, peace, and fulfillment. God wants you to experience this too. Written for both married couples and couples in marriage preparation, I hope this book will help you obtain all of these blessings.

You have been given the wonderful opportunity of becoming one with someone here on earth through your relationship with your spouse. Your ability to personally transform—placing higher priority on your spouse's own needs over your own—will allow the two of you to become one, united in marriage. This will serve you well; it is your personal preparation for heaven. The cornerstone on this spiritual path to a successful marriage will be *your top two priorities in life: the first will be making your relationship with God your top priority, and the second will be your relationship with your spouse.* All other relationships, activities, career objectives, financial goals, and intellectual pursuits must be prioritized after these two—*without exception.*

Through the process of becoming one together in the Lord, two people can have a great marriage of meaning, fulfillment, and joy. As Genesis 2:24 states: "That is why a man leaves his father and mother and clings to his wife, and the two of them become one body." Being united as one body, you and your spouse can live complete, whole, and integrated lives, connected to what God wants for the both of you and for your marriage. By accepting Jesus' life and His love for you as *the* model for your marriage, you both have the opportunity to begin understanding the ultimate truth: *by loving and serving each other, you are also loving and serving the Lord, and you will ultimately become one with Him.*

God wants you to have a happy, love-filled, successful marriage and family life. The purpose of this book is to help you accomplish this. Throughout, specific scriptures from the New American Bible (NAB) translation are offered to illuminate the teachings and lead your development. The advice I will give you is primarily based on my understanding of Christian scriptural principles, framed by my experiences as a deacon in the Roman Catholic Church, spiritual advisor, husband, and father. Though written from a Catholic Christian perspective, these principles apply to all persons seeking a happy, fulfilling life and marriage regardless of specific religious denomination. I will share many deep insights into marriage success that I have learned from my experiences working with hundreds of couples through the years, as well as from my own forty-seven-years of marriage.

AN OVERVIEW OF THE CHAPTERS

- Chapter One: *Finding Willingness to Change* launches into my personal testimony: how my self-focus, misplaced priorities, and lack of awareness of my wife's feelings brought about the greatest crisis in our marriage and lives. It describes my moments of revelation that my top two priorities in life needed to be God and Elaine, in that order.
- Chapter Two: *Making a Personal Transformation* reflects on how the act of becoming humbled and transformed was an emotional walk of fire that I needed to take to save my marriage. This chapter will illustrate how God took Elaine and me and our unhealthy and doomed marriage, challenged both our hearts and resolve, and then transformed us so that we could eventually live as a thriving, happy, and loving couple becoming one in the Lord. Ultimately, the message that I want to share with you is that personal transformation is not only possible, it is essential to leading a fulfilling life. If you and your spouse both agree to a personal transformation and put Christ at

the center of your lives and marriage, you can have a wonderful relationship.

- Chapter Three: *Sharing the Fruit of the Spirit* explores the fruit of the Spirit as evidence of your having made a personal transformation. You will be asked to look at who is really in control of your life—you or God? This chapter then discusses the blessing of your spouse's feedback as a means for discerning the good "spiritual" fruit from the desires of the flesh. In closing, when your life reflects the fruit, it lets others see the power of the Holy Spirit working in your life and in your actions. This will serve as an inspiration to them and to their own personal transformation and growth.

- Chapter Four: *The Two Shall Become One* addresses the topics of two becoming one, the issues involving love, and the challenges to becoming "one body," and how to put the concepts into practice. This chapter begins by defining "spiritual unions" in terms of two people becoming one body in the eyes of the Lord. This understanding is integral to the Catholic Church and interpreted in the Catholic wedding vows. For spouses to really commit to one another, love is then defined as a decision rather than a feeling. Once the decision to love has been made, God will teach you, through your spouse, how to love without conditions, to forgive, to change, and to grow. By then asking the question, "Why isn't everyone having a great marriage?" the chapter explores the issues associated with addictions and distractions, "judgmentalism," unwillingness to change, and the loss of faith in marriage. This chapter closes with the discussion of how working to understand and live the Word of God will set the foundation for the great marriage that you are meant to have.

- Chapter Five: *A Balanced Life* looks at the categories of Family, Intellect, Social Activities, Health, Economics, and Spirituality (FISHES) to explore how balancing these key activities in life helps focus and create synergy between each of the categories. By answering detailed questions offered in each of the FISHES categories, you will be able to drill down to your specific behavior traits and identify where you want to make improvements. The FISHES exercise will help you determine overall how satisfied you are with your life at any point in time and to gauge whether it is well balanced.

- Chapter Six: *A Blueprint for Marriage* looks at how you and your spouse can develop a "plan" for building a happy and successful marriage. This chapter explores some of the different general needs and requirements that men and women have in regards to their married life. It also suggests some of the more effective activities and efforts you and your spouse can do to positively reinforce your Christian principles.

- Chapter Seven: *Dealing with Life's Difficulties* discusses how to properly deal with the difficulties that surely arise in marriage and in life. It will suggest practical how-to approaches to challenges such as handling a lack of quality "couple time," dealing with negative emotions, managing conflicts, improving communications, overcoming resentments and lingering past pain, and learning to work together for the good of the marriage. This chapter offers direction on how to take personal responsibility for achieving success.

- Chapter Eight: *A Great Marriage Is Life Changing* explores how having a great marriage alters the course of your life and the lives of those around you, including your children, in very meaningful and tangible ways. By reviewing many of the key spiritual principles outlined in this book, it should become clear that having a great marriage—as well as a great life—is within your grasp. Once you ask God for courage and strength, and then commit to taking personal responsibility for the quality of your marriage and relationships, "The Spiritual Steps to a Great Marriage" laid out in this chapter will help give you the roadmap, action items, and tools to transform an unfulfilled marriage into a shared, spiritual, joy-filled journey. At the closing of this book, you will be challenged to envision the quality of your life and marriage once you've become inspired to offer your spouse unconditional love.

FINDING A WILLINGNESS TO CHANGE

A JOURNEY IN FAITH

Looking back over the life Elaine and I have lived together to the very beginning, ours seemed a perfect courtship. We were both raised as good Catholic kids. Elaine spent all twelve grades in the Catholic school of our town. I attended the public school but took all the programs of catechism. As a young boy, my live-in grandparents brought me to church every Sunday morning *and* every Friday night, grooming me to be the lone priest of their five grandchildren. And yes, I even went to novenas. Ours was a routine that included a cowboy movie after Friday night services, which led me to think that Gene Autry and Roy Rogers were somehow affiliated with church.

A few years later, when I became a teenager, my grandmother passed away, easing the pressure on me to become a priest. By my senior year in high school, the time finally came for me to make the decision on what to do about the seminary. I chose Texas A&M University instead. Unfortunately for me, both institutions—the seminary and

Texas A&M—had a common thread: no girls allowed. I began to pray, "God, I chose this place. Please bring girls here to A&M!"

Being the first in my family to go to college, some relatives and friends told me that college would be a waste of time. Their view was that I'd have a far greater jump on life by getting a job right away. It was 1960, an era when approximately only 20 percent of young people pursued education beyond high school. At the time, Texas A&M was a fairly large university, having 10,000 students enrolled. Today the school educates over 40,000 students each year, approximately half of which are females. Considering that my older son met his wife on that campus, I'd say my prayers were eventually answered—for him and many other young men. *I may not have been the only one praying.*

The education I received as a young man was excellent, with one exception: I had never actually read the entire Bible. Prior to Vatican II, most Catholics were not encouraged to read the Bible for various reasons. We were told that the priests would read the Bible and then interpret the scripture for us. The Vatican II documents encouraged the bishops of each country to translate the entire Bible into the language of their people, thus attempting to make knowledge of God more available by encouraging everyone to read scripture for themselves. Led by the Holy Spirit, the bishops said that getting Bibles into the hands of the people was critical.

The church's teachings have always encouraged developing scriptural knowledge. In his introduction to the book of the Prophet Isaiah, Saint Jerome wrote, "[I obey] the precepts of Christ who says 'examine scriptures.'" Matthew's Gospel 7:7 says, "Ask and it will be given to you; seek and you will find; knock and the door will be opened to you." Later in Matthew's Gospel, Jesus responds to a group of Sadducees attempting to trick him by saying, "You are misled because you do not know the scriptures or the power of God" (Matthew 22:29). In his introduction to Isaiah, Saint Jerome even clearly states, "For if, according to the apostle Paul, Christ is the power of God and the wisdom of God and who does not know scripture does not know the power or the wisdom of God, then ignorance of scripture is ignorance of Christ" (Saint Jerome, Commentariorum in Isaiam libri xviii prol.: PL 24, 17b).

Therefore, putting this approach into practice, the more we know about Christ, the stronger our faith, the more Christ-like our lives will be.

AND THEY LIVED HAPPILY EVER AFTER?

When Elaine and I first started seeing each other, I was a senior in college. Though we had known each other in high school, we had not actually dated. It was during the holiday season in 1963, and I was looking for a date for Christmas Eve. A good friend of mine suggested that I contact Elaine. Anxiously, I called her up to see if she would like to go to Midnight Mass. We had a great conversation; however, she said that she already had a date for that night. We continued chatting and eventually decided to make it one big fun event by double dating. That turned out to be one of the best Midnight Masses! We all had a blast that night, and I became intrigued by Elaine. She seemed to be everything that I was looking for and fit the list of all the qualities that I was seeking in a potential wife. Smart, attractive, funny, social, Catholic—Elaine seemed to be the perfect match. After that Christmas Eve, I asked Elaine if she would like to go out—just the two of us this time, though.

Feeling the spark, we dated for several months and then were married in 1964. A few years later, we had two young boys, and from my perspective, things seemed to be going smoothly. What I thought was a high enough goal—to be better than 50 percent of the married men—turned out to be a low standard when 50 percent of marriages were ending in divorce. In line with the times, I was putting minimal effort into having a great marriage. My priorities were not in the correct order; worldly and selfish desires were always first.

Even after Vatican II encouraged the reading of Scripture and the opportunities for me to understand the Bible opened up, I still chose not to study the Bible. My interests were elsewhere. Specifically, I had not read 1 Timothy 6:10, which states, "For the love of money is the root of all evils, and some people in their desire for it have strayed from the faith and have pierced themselves with many pains."

And quite honestly, I did love money! My plan after graduating from college with a mathematics degree was to set out to change the world and become a millionaire. Please understand that there is nothing wrong with having a goal of becoming a millionaire as long as you respect that *the love* of money is the root of all evil. We all know that money can be a powerful resource when used wisely and for a greater good.

The problem I had in my early years was that I put my desires before God. My desire to get ahead was my primary goal and top priority; I had confused God with my own personal ambition—*God was not at the center of my life.* Advancing in my career, making money, and having professional success were my driving goals. All else were merely distractions, and that included both God and my wife. In fact, my wife and my kids were not even in the top five of my priorities. I was a workaholic and knew of no other way. As Matthew 6:21 states, "For where your treasure is, there also will your heart be."

Satan attempts to trick you into prioritizing other things before God. In my case it was worldly desires and my own ambition. I was not living by the Ten Commandments—rather, I was living by the commandments that I had created for myself. Matthew 4:8–10 states:

> Then the devil took him up to a very high mountain, and showed him all the kingdoms of the world in their magnificence, and he said to him, "All these I shall give to you, if you will prostrate yourself and worship me." At this, Jesus said to him, "Get away, Satan! It is written: 'The Lord, your God, shall you worship and him alone shall you serve.'"

Because serving God was not my top priority, I was susceptible to listening to the lies of Satan. In fact, in my ignorance at the time, I was not sure there even was a

Satan. Once worldly desires became my top priority, I did not even really believe there was such a place as hell.

Attending Sunday mass became like an insurance policy, only so that I could get into heaven—still one of my goals. Aside from my weekly hour of attending and commenting on the content and the quality of the service, I had minimized any involvement at church. I was okay with doing what I thought was the minimum required to get my ticket into heaven. I was pretty sure that, even after Vatican II, the priests and administrators could run the church without my help. I was only interested in making money and getting ahead.

Though committed to my marriage, I was not totally committed to my wife—I was a workaholic. Following the path of being a good husband and "responsible workaholic," I dedicated myself to becoming a millionaire, taking priority over all else. I thought that money would buy our happiness. If I was able to buy things for my wife and kids—fulfilling that version of the American Dream—then I must be meeting their needs. Why wouldn't they be happy?

Then after about seven years, I came home one day to that beautiful wife who had passed all of my tests. She said, "Tommy, I want a divorce."

BUT I'M HAPPY!

Elaine then explained that she wanted to divorce me because she felt I didn't love her. My first reaction to this was, "Yes, of course I love you!" In fact, after thinking about this further, I told her that she was one of the few people that I actually did love. *How could my perception of our relationship be so off?* Then after deeper consideration, I began wondering how all other people thought of me if the one person that I truly loved didn't think I loved her at all.

Leading up to that day, my wife had obviously put a great deal of thought into her decision to divorce me. She told me that she felt treated like an object—as I did not love her—but rather loved the things that she could do for me, such as always having meals prepared on time, cleaning up after me, and taking care of our children. She felt that she was doing all the things that a maid or a personal assistant could do for me and that we did not have that much-needed personal connection. In addition, she felt pressured to do as she was told and not to argue about it. She wanted more out of our relationship.

Elaine's request for a divorce and the feelings she shared deeply concerned me. I was about to become just like some of my friends—divorced—*something that I initially set out not to be.*

When a spouse asks for a divorce, it is probably not the couple's first conversation about their problems. In the first several years of our relationship, there had been signs of problems that ultimately led up to the divorce request. However, I ignored the signs for seven years because *I was happy.*

I was focused on my own priorities, which were money and career first—not God first and Elaine second.

My rationale was that working was good; the more I worked, the more money I would make, and the better I could provide for my family. I always felt justified in anything I did because I was providing for them and their futures. *Certainly they must know that I love them or else I would not be working as much as I am,* I rationalized. This mind-set of commitment to work and career above all else had been passed down through my family for generations. So while I was indeed providing my wife and children with sustenance, what I did not offer them much of was my time and involvement. Although I thought my love for Elaine was apparent, I didn't understand what it meant to love her in the ways that she needed to be loved.

Elaine had not thought about what would happen after she divorced me. She didn't care. She was not looking out for tomorrow. She wanted to end the pain, the loneliness, and the neglect right then. She wanted out of our marriage and would worry about tomorrow tomorrow. The way she had envisioned it playing out, she would initially leave the kids with me, as she didn't yet have an income. I would then hire someone to take care of them. Her plan was to find a job, and then once she got back on her feet, she would bring the boys to live with her. After two-plus years of reflection and consideration, Elaine felt there was no other way to escape the isolation and misery she felt in our marriage.

All that time, I had been completely clueless about what was troubling her. Now looking back, all the warning signs were there that something needed to change. None of the issues, however, were ever addressed or discussed. I went about my personal pursuits of money and career. Unfortunately, my wife and children were fairly low on my priority list. Clearly, I had not yet understood Matthew 6:24, which states:

> No one can serve two masters. He will either hate one and love the other, or be devoted to one and despise the other. You cannot serve God and mammon.

And I certainly had not appreciated what Timothy 6:10 says: "For the love of money is the root of all evil."

The love of money had caused me to dislike and separate myself from other people. In particular, it had distanced me from my wife and family. I've since learned that in many marriages, the love of money can bring extreme conflict—both for irresponsible spending habits and the misguided appreciation or hoarding of money. Money can also become an issue when it is lent to family or friends. If the borrower is unable or slow to pay the debt back, it can cause bitterness or anger. Having now worked with many couples through the years to improve troubled marriages and relationships, a common theme I've seen is that without God at the center of their lives, something else will be their focus.

Was the focus I had on money at that time driving my wife and children away from me? At that point in my marriage, I just didn't know.

SINKING IN REALITY

When my wife asked for a divorce, I was shocked. My first reaction was, "From me? But I went to college. I have a successful career. You have a home, a car, and beautiful kids. I know that I am better than at least half of those other guys out there."

However, the times had changed. When the divorce rate was 50 percent, simply being better than half of all men who were married was no longer good enough. The world had changed around us. I like to tell the younger generations that prior to 1960, women felt they essentially *had* to stay with their husbands regardless of how they were treated. Over the last half century, the social and economic norms have dramatically evolved. Men actually have to behave and act in ways that they *deserve* their spouses now! Wives do not have to stay with their husbands for economic reasons, and the world no longer looks down upon women who leave miserable, neglectful, abusive, or unloving marriages.

So at that moment of surprise over Elaine's request for a divorce, I felt how the disciple Peter must have felt in the story of Jesus and him walking on the water. As you recall, when Peter began to lose faith in what Jesus had asked him to do, he sank into the sea and cried out for help. This story is reflected in Matthew 14:22–33:

> Then he made the disciples get into the boat and precede him to the other side, while he dismissed the crowds. After doing so, he went up on the mountain by himself to pray. When it was evening he was

there alone. Meanwhile the boat, already a few miles offshore, was being tossed about by the waves, for the wind was against it. During the fourth watch of the night, he came toward them, walking on the sea. When the disciples saw him walking on the sea they were terrified. "It is a ghost," they said, and they cried out in fear. At once (Jesus) spoke to them, "Take courage, it is I; do not be afraid." Peter said to him in reply, "Lord, if it is you, command me to come to you on the water." He said, "Come." Peter got out of the boat and began to walk on the water toward Jesus. But when he saw how (strong) the wind was he became frightened; and, beginning to sink, he cried out, "Lord, save me!" Immediately Jesus stretched out his hand and caught him, and said to him, "O you of little faith, why did you doubt?" After they got into the boat, the wind died down. Those who were in the boat did him homage, saying, "Truly, you are the Son of God."

Peter was a bold man, being the only disciple to jump out of the boat and to begin walking toward Jesus across the water. This much took tremendous faith. But upon hearing the howling of the winds and feeling the water, he became frightened, questioned his belief in being able to walk on water, and he started to sink. Feeling overwhelmed and powerless, Peter called out for Jesus to save him, "Lord, save me!" *And that is how I felt in my marriage.*

A MOMENT OF REVELATION

Like Peter, I prayed that God would intervene in my own life. Up until that point, I had rarely gone out of my way or done anything special to be a great husband or to improve the quality of my marriage. My wife needed much more from me than I had even thought of offering. So in those revealing moments of Elaine's inner pain, I finally began to understand that she wanted me to change. However, I didn't know where to begin.

Some of my friends, family, and coworkers had been divorced, and I was about to be just like them. In earnest, I said, "Honey, let's not get a divorce. Let's do something to fix this." Knowing marriage renewal to be a significant commitment, we both recognized that it would take much more than a quick fix to do the trick.

Clearly, there were quite a few issues that we had never addressed up to that point in our marriage. So I turned to God, confessing to Him that I was clueless as to what was wrong. I felt that Elaine was a wonderful wife, and up until that moment of truth, I thought our marriage was fine. I could see, though, that *our* problem was not *her* problem. Out of desperation, out of wanting to save my marriage, I began to recognize that I needed to be willing to change. I asked God, "What do I need to do to become the husband she wants me to be?"

PRIORITIES: PUT GOD FIRST IN YOUR LIFE

Well, God heard my prayers and decided to intervene. Sitting at home one night, I got a knock on my door. It happened to be a friend of mine named Dr. Peters. He said, "Tom, I've been driving all the way from Amarillo to Galveston, and God told me to stop at your house." I was amazed. That was the first time I had ever met someone with whom God actually talked, so of course I invited him in! Looking at me directly, in a soft yet serious tone, Dr. Peters said, "Let me tell you why I think God wanted me to be here. I too was having problems with my marriage and God helped me. Here, take this book. It is something I think you should read." We then prayed together before he continued on his journey.

The book was *A New Song* by Pat Boone. Pat had been one of my idols when I was a teenager in the 1950s. The man had style and class, he sang love songs, and all the girls seemed to have crushes on him. Well, that night I stayed up for hours reading the whole book—it was a relatively short book, but I was a slow reader. The story focused on Pat, his wife, and their four daughters. Pat's wife also had asked for a divorce. And just like my predicament, Pat didn't know what to do or how to deal with it. It was spooky because it was just like reading my own life story.

Hoping to save his marriage, Pat had also prayed for guidance and direction. He soon began to see that he was moving away from God in his life. He then took inventory of his priorities and made the commitment to put God first in his life. Once he began living his life that way, allowing the Holy Spirit to lead him and transform him, his marriage improved.

After I finished reading *A New Song* that night, I thanked God for His effective response to my question about what I should do to save my marriage. Like Pat Boone, I learned that I would need to assess and realign all my priorities. Definitively, I must put God first in my life, and then let all my other decisions, actions, and reactions reflect that commitment.

GOD'S INTERVENTION: LOVE YOUR ENEMIES

Before that day when I committed to make my relationship with God priority number one, I believed that one would need to be *holy* before they could be one with the LORD. The mistake I made was in not realizing that He simply wants us to put Him first in our lives. God then helps us to clean up our acts over the course of our lifetimes. So up until rearranging my priorities, I had attempted to go about it the hard way, going it alone, and trying to act holy.

In my pursuit of *holiness,* I had developed a habit of passing judgment, especially on those I considered enemies and people I didn't like. I had not yet grasped a real understanding of John 3:17, which tells us, "For God did not send his Son into the world to condemn the world, but that the world might be saved through Him." And in my ignorance—or even arrogance—I wanted to believe that God had sent me to judge others. Matthew 5:44 was lost on me: "But I say to you, love your enemies, and pray for those who persecute you." Thus, how would it have been possible for me to love my enemies while being so impassioned to judge them?

Rather than sending me word that I was to serve as His anointed critic of mankind, God then sent me a man named Kent. Working in the office next to mine, Kent was the first person I ever met who carried a Bible to work in his coat. At that time, I also was reading the Scriptures, hoping to learn about how I might change in ways that would reflect my newfound commitment to God.

One day I joined Kent in his office. "I am trying to put God first in my life but I seem to be hitting a barrier," I said.

Kent was quick to ask, "Do you hate anyone, Tommy?"

I said, "Yes, several people! In fact, my friend (who we'll call "Bob") who owes me money is at the top of the list, and he's borrowed from me twice!" (Of course, to lend to a person twice without being paid back really says something more about me than Bob, but that's another story.)

Kent pulled out his Bible from his coat, turned first to 1 John 4:20–21, and read:

> If anyone says, "I love God," but hates his brother, he is a liar; for whoever does not love a brother whom he has seen cannot love God whom he has not seen. This is the commandment we have from him: whoever loves God must also love his brother.

Simply put, the instruction that God is giving is this: Whoever loves God must also love his brothers and sisters. *Being a Christian means learning to love all others.*

I had made an important first step by being willing to change. I had also grown from loving no one to loving only my wife and sons. However, my scope was still somewhat limited on what it meant to love others. It had not yet dawned on me that God's devotion to us knows no limits and that the LORD loves us just the way that we are, with all of our faults. What God was telling me that day was, "If you want to love Me, you must learn how to love everyone. Learn to not hate. Learn to forgive your family and friends (even those who owe you money). *Once you've learned how to accept and love all people as they actually are, then you and I will be one.*" This was an awakening.

The funny thing is, until then, becoming "one in the LORD" had never really been one of my goals. In fact, the only church-related goal I had ever set was to get into heaven—even if I had to sneak in! And so I thought I had that covered.

But now I was looking for more than just finding a way into heaven—I wanted the LORD to save my marriage. I had already taken a huge step by committing to make Him my first priority. And now here was Kent showing me scriptural proof that God wants me to love everybody. He turned to John 13:34 and read, "Love one another. As I have loved you, so you should love one another." Obviously that commandment was one I had not yet grasped.

That afternoon in Kent's office, I prayed, "LORD, I'm ready to change. If I'm not yet fully willing under Your guidance, at least help me be willing to be willing. Please soften my heart and strengthen my will. Outside my own family, there aren't many people I currently love. However, I am going to start by forgiving everyone. I am also going to forgive anyone who owes me money, including my friend Bob, who made no effort to repay. I don't even want the money anymore. No longer will the love of money hold me back. Please teach me how to love people the right way, Lord. I want to learn how to love without judging."

Without my knowing, that same afternoon Elaine made an appointment with a lawyer for the following week to begin the divorce proceedings. Though she had seen my personal struggles and witnessed a lot of action and effort on my part, she had not seen the changes and transformation I had promised her. Quite honestly, until that day there would have been little chance that she could have seen those results. It was only that day that I began to understand what had been my biggest obstacle: my love was conditional and I loved very few people. But now, as I asked for God's help in learning to love unconditionally and offered Him my commitment to practice forgiveness, I could sense the winds of change stirring on my horizon. The journey had begun.

A PERSONAL TRANSFORMATION

BEING OPEN TO CHANGE

As many of us know, old habits often die hard—especially when they are our own. Bad habits and self-focus can become sacred cows blocking our paths to becoming one in the Lord. Take me for example—I was once the poster child for workaholism, self-centeredness, selfishness, and the love of money. Despite my attempts to make Him adjust to my desires and lifestyle, God was not the one who needed to change. God has been the way He is for an eternity and will continue to be. Hebrews 13:8 clearly defines Christ's unchanging nature: "Jesus Christ is the same yesterday, today, and forever."

However, once I became willing and open to change, as guided by the Scripture, the Holy Spirit began helping me to become a better person and to be transformed. By making God my number one priority and my spouse my number two priority, He began guiding me through the necessary personal changes I needed to make to have a personal relationship with Him, a successful marriage, and a happy life.

Remember, the only person you can change is yourself. As Jesus told us in Matthew 7:3, "Why do you notice the splinter in your brother's eye, but do not perceive the wooden beam in your own eye?" When a person does not want to change *who they are,* they often take it upon themselves to try changing the person *who their spouse is.* Believe it or not, I actually remember praying, *Please God, change my wife!* What an easy solution that would seem to be. Fortunately, I learned that it doesn't work that way. Asking for guidance and insight, I modified my prayer to L ORD *, please help* me *to change.*

Once you become willing to change, you also allow people who care about your growth the right to help you become a better person, and no one has more invested in seeing you grow than your spouse! Are there two or three things you could change about yourself each year that would help you to become more like Jesus? Try asking your spouse for their opinion on this. If your goal is to become one together in the L ORD, and not just more like each other, then Jesus should be your common model. As the Holy Spirit begins working in your marriage, you will both become more like Jesus. Thus, give your spouse the right to help you change. Otherwise, any suggestions they may make to help you spiritually grow could seem like criticism or nagging—when it may actually be God speaking directly to you.

By giving your spouse the right to help you change, you are also demonstrating your love—and people respond to love. As you take the responsibility to make the necessary changes within yourself, your spouse will recognize you adapting to their needs and will become more open to change themselves. Your marriage and the world around you will come into alignment with the new you.

SHARING CHRIST WITH OTHERS

Remember that fateful Friday whereby I confessed to my friend Kent that I was willing to change? Well, the truth of the matter was that God knew that I wasn't yet really willing to change. But however—and this is the big "but however"—God could see that I was now willing to be willing. My intentions were sincere. By reading the scriptures, I was now trying to understand how I could apply God's teachings to my life.

I had never before shared Christ with a single person. Frankly, I felt that I had nothing to share. But it was time for God to once again intervene in my life.

On the Sunday of that same weekend as my come-to-Jesus meeting with Kent, there was a knock at our door. To my surprise, it was Bob—my friend who owed me money. Let's just say that until that day, I did not exactly have loving thoughts or joyous feelings for him. Once upon a time, the man had borrowed money from me and had never made any motion toward paying me back. Today was somehow different, though—he was carrying a Bible. I had not seen the man in several years and, believe me, the last time I saw him, he may have been carrying quite a few things, though none of which were Bibles.

To my utter amazement, Bob told me that day he had come over to ask for my forgiveness and pay me every dime that he owed me. *Whoa!* I dared not analyze why God was sending me messages through a repentant friend right on my doorstep.

We then hugged each other for the first time in our lives. It's probably unnecessary to mention that he and I had never been too close. In fact, one of the last things Bob told my wife before we got married was, "Don't marry him." Bob had had a series of challenges in his life, and his alcohol and drug problems had played a factor in each of his five marriages.

On that fateful Sunday he came to make amends, Bob shared with me what God was doing in his life. Once he had put God first in his life, it became much easier for him to get his act together and to gain personal control. He then shared with Elaine and me what finding God had meant to his overall happiness and purpose in life. Actively involving God in all aspects of his life had filled his soul with purpose and a love for all.

So at that moment, he and I prayed together for the first time in our lives. We both asked forgiveness for our petty concerns and our self-centeredness in Jesus' name. Romans 10:9–10 states:

> For, if you confess with your mouth that Jesus is Lord and believe in your heart that God raised him from the dead, you will be saved. For one believes with the heart and so is justified, and one confesses with the mouth and so is saved.

I prayed that day and confessed, and I continue to confess, that Jesus is Lord. I believe that He was resurrected for the love of me and all humankind. I know that by following Him and through the promises of the Bible, my baptism, and my confirmation, I will live eternally in heaven. Because of the faith I have in my destiny, I am of value to myself and others as a witness for Christ.

Bob then asked me what I knew about the Holy Spirit. We addressed the question by looking at some relevant passages in the Scripture. We reflected on John 14:26–27, which explains that Jesus never intended to leave us alone. Rather, He sent the Holy Spirit to be with us as a guide and teacher:

> The Advocate, the holy Spirit that the Father will send in my name—he will teach you everything and remind you of all that (I) told you. Peace I leave with you; my peace I give to you. Not as the world gives do I give it to you. Do not let your hearts be troubled or afraid.

In addition, we read together the message of a new beginning that Acts 1:4–5 teaches us:

> To wait for the promise of the Father about which you have heard me speak; for John baptized with water, but in a few days you will be baptized with the Holy Spirit.

And Luke 11:13:

> If you then, who are wicked, know how to give good gifts to your children, how much more will the Father in heaven give the holy Spirit to those who ask him?

Bob then asked me if I wanted the Holy Spirit active in my life. He was reaching out and offering the gift of healing, as described in James 5:19–20:

> My brothers, if anyone among you should stray from the truth and someone bring him back, he should know that whoever brings back a sinner from the error of his way will save his soul from death and will cover a multitude of sins.

I had received the Holy Spirit at baptism when I became a child of God and at confirmation when I said I would follow Jesus, be part of the body of Christ, and do my part to share God's love with the world. But I had not allowed the Holy Spirit to be active in my life. I was not listening to God's directions to me. Just as I had prayed with Bob and renewed my commitment for Jesus to be Lord of my life and at the center of my life, I prayed that the Holy Spirit would lead and guide me. I asked God to renew His Holy Spirit within me. I prayed that His Holy Spirit would transform me, just as He had transformed the disciples at Pentecost in Acts 2:1–5:

> When the time for Pentecost was fulfilled, they were all in one place together. And suddenly there came from the sky a noise like a strong driving wind, and it filled the entire house in which they were. Then there appeared to them tongues as of fire, which parted and came to rest on each one of them. And they were all filled with the holy Spirit and began to speak in different tongues, as the Spirit enabled them

to proclaim. Now there were devout Jews from every nation under heaven staying in Jerusalem.

I prayed for a new Pentecost in my life. God answered my prayer. That day I had a new beginning, and every day since then, I ask for the help of the Father, the Son, and Holy Spirit. I turned to Elaine, who was watching me, and I said with a big smile, "Honey, this is what *you* need."

She said, "Can I say a prayer?" We all bowed our heads.

She said, "God, protect me from my husband and our friend Bob—"

The revelations I had with both Kent and Bob came just in the nick of time, as my wife saw for the first time that my priorities had changed. She canceled the appointment she had set with her lawyer that next day. The change that she had prayed for was happening right before her eyes. Not even Doubting Thomas himself could deny that kind of a transformation.

In John 8:31, Jesus said to those who had chosen to believe in Him, "If you remain in My Word, you will truly be my disciples, and you will know the truth and the truth will set you free."

That weekend, I recognized the power and the utter joy of living as a disciple of Jesus. The truth that set us both free was our decision to make God first in our personal lives and first in our marriage. Once I made that choice, I really began to learn what it meant to love people—not only my wife and kids, but also my coworkers and, oh yes, even a friend who owed me money. By asking and accepting Christ into our hearts and allowing the Holy Spirit to inspire our transformation, my wife and I began the process of turning what had been a worthless marriage into a priceless one.

CHOOSING THE RIGHT PATH IN LIFE

I, you, and all of us want to ride down the chartered road to a happy eternity. However, this amazing path to eternal life in heaven is not just a single lane; it is designed to be a shared passageway. By taking time with others, especially your spouse, reaching out and helping them along their journey, you will be ensuring that your own path will be clear. Paul stresses this analogy of shared spiritual travel and mutual benefit in Romans 14:13:

> Then let us no longer judge one another, but rather resolve never to put a stumbling block or hindrance in the way of a brother.

Our faith calls us to believe in the existence and workings of God, Jesus Christ, and the Holy Spirit. We must also believe in the existence of Satan and evil. Some people do not believe that Satan even exists—and that plays right into Satan's game. Satan can guide us down the wrong path without us even realizing it. Jesus makes this clear when he tells us in Matthew 13:19:

> The seed sown on the path is the one who hears the word of the kingdom without understanding it, and the evil one comes and steals away what was sown in his heart.

Though God loves each one of us equally, salvation is only granted to those who choose to pursue His path. Unfortunately, though, some people believe that making this choice is not necessary and nothing is required for entrance to heaven. That is Satan working to make us complacent. Satan is stealing our opportunity for joy.

The good news is that God provides His Son, Jesus Christ, as our path to salvation and the Holy Spirit to guide us along our search for everlasting joy and salvation. John 14: 6 says, "I am the way and the truth and the life. No one comes to the Father except through me."

The decision to follow Jesus is your own personal responsibility. In great marriages that are alive with the Holy Spirit, both spouses support, encourage, and give each other a hand in making the changes necessary to follow in the pathway of Jesus and grow in their faith.

Even when you are following the right path, though, there still may be a tendency to blame others for your own weaknesses. Just as in Matthew 7:3, you may sometimes be tempted to complain about the speck in your spouse's eye while ignoring the log in your own eye. Rather than praying for your spouse to change, pray for God to change you. The only one you can transform is yourself. Remember to pray the simple yet powerful prayer, "Lord, change me"—and not "Lord, change my spouse." With this, you are taking all the responsibility upon yourself to affect change in the relationship, asking for God's help to find the necessary courage, and believing that love from you will transform others and draw them to God.

LORD, CHANGE ME

Throughout the years, I continued to pray the "Lord, change me" prayer. Oh yes, I dutifully remembered to not ask the Lord to change my spouse. However, this did not stop my asking the Lord to change other people, particularly my rebellious teenage son.

Over months my prayers continued, as did my son continue his commitment to be challenging. One day, the Lord said to me, "Hey, Tom. What about you?" My immediate response was, "Lord, I am a Deacon. I have a great marriage. People love me. I'm working at the church. That boy is the one who needs to change—he is the one who is the rebellious teenager." But the Lord said again, "What about you?" I finally began sensing that God was trying to tell me something. So, reluctantly at first, I began refocusing my prayer to just "Okay, Lord, please change me."

Immediately, I started observing a few things. I noticed that the only time my son and I really talked was when I was correcting him, angry with him, or trying to straighten him out. Hoping to turn things around, I told my son that I wanted to begin meeting with him every week. That was a tough sell because, as you can imagine, he certainly did not want to start meeting with me!

Knowing that our first meeting needed to set the proper tone, I opened our talk by apologizing for my actions, for not loving him unconditionally, and for not making it clear that I loved him so much that I was willing to lay down my life for him. I said, "Son, I would like for us to start meeting every week. I will begin by telling you I love you and then about why I follow Jesus. God gave you to your mother and me to raise until you become an adult. Once you do become an adult, you will then have an adult decision to make. You will have to decide if you also want to follow Christ and begin your journey to eternal life in heaven. It will be your decision. Your mother and I cannot make that decision for you. But I do want to tell you why I follow Christ. It is the right decision, and I hope you make it as well. I'll always be available to you if you'd like to talk with me about it."

So from that day forward, I met with my son every week, loving him and talking with him as a non-angry man. I also began making a special prayer for him every day, and I told him so. When he asked for what I was praying, I said, "Well, the first thing I pray is that you live to be twenty-five."

He then asked, "Why is that, Dad?"

"Well, because I'm worried about you making it to twenty-five," I answered. "And number two, if by the grace of God you do make it to be twenty-five, I believe that you are going to realize the value of the advice I've been giving you, and that God is active in your life."

In working to develop this new relationship with my son, I reflected on Luke 11:13: "If you then, who are wicked, know how to give good gifts to your children, how much more will the Father in heaven give the holy Spirit to those who ask him?"

This first gift I offered to my son was the sharing of my reasons for following Christ. My faith was a gift given to me, and I wanted to share that tremendous gift with my son. The second gift I wanted to give him was to be accessible and to have an open mind and ear whereby he could feel comfortable discussing with me his personal thoughts and feelings on spiritual matters. The third gift I offered was a demonstration of my respect of him as a growing and developing man of Christian faith. He gratefully accepted these three gifts, and over the course of our talks, there were many more that were shared between us both.

As we continued to meet and work on our relationship, there were times when situations required us to take some actions. I'll share with you a moving example: One day upon coming home from work, my wife met me at the door. I could tell something had unsettled her. She then told me about an incident that occurred at the house that afternoon where our son, the one with whom I'd been working, had been very disrespectful to her. Seeing how important an issue this was to my wife, with drastic measures being called for, I phoned my parents and asked them if my son could go live with them. They agreed.

I then called my son in for a meeting. I told him, "Son, I love you, and I want you to live with us. However, you must make a decision regarding your actions from this day forward. You cannot be disrespectful to your mother. That is something completely under your control, and it is your decision. So in the morning, you tell me whether you can honor a commitment to respect your mother. Otherwise, I am prepared to drive you to your grandparents' house, and you can live with them. From now on, if you want to shout at somebody, call me. I'll meet with you, and you can say anything that you want to say. As your father you know I can be a tough, crusty guy, and you can talk with me about any of your issues. But you will not ever again treat your mother as you did."

Fortunately for all of us, that was the last day that he was ever disrespectful to his mother. He made the decision to live with us, and he kept his commitment to appreciate the feelings of his mother. I thought, *Praise God!* He began showing his mother respect and still does to this day. I was so proud of him for taking the personal responsibility for his own transformation. My son recognized that he was the one who needed to change—and not his parents. That was a life-changing day where he learned to pull the log out of his own eye.

The lesson learned is that God wants us to look at ourselves first and pray for our own transformation before wishing others to change. Rather than becoming frustrated and upset when dealing with anyone who may not think or act how you would like them to, *control what you actually can control: your intentions and your actions.* Ask, "Lord, please let me act from a place of love and let the necessary changes happen within me."

SHARING THE FRUIT OF THE SPIRIT

THE SPIRIT VERSUS THE FLESH

Many years ago, before I faced the spiritual crisis of potentially losing my wife and family, I thought that I had my life pretty well figured out. Yes, of course I knew at the time I could probably change a thing or two and perhaps even try to be less judgmental. However, any kind of wholesale changes in me and what made me tick certainly didn't seem necessary. What I didn't know at the time was just how desperate the situation in my marriage and in my soul had actually become. I was completely ignorant of how spiritually empty my life had been and how it was slowly destroying my marriage. Left unchecked, it would have eventually destroyed me as well.

My revelation came at that moment of reckoning as my wife told me she had had enough and was going to seek a divorce. Right then I peered into the dark abyss of my life and soul and realized that my whole perception of what constituted my "happy marriage," focusing only on being a good provider, had been a selfish lie.

Working with my wife through the life-altering changes I knew were needed, brought on by this insight, a few clear prophetic messages began to speak to me over time:

- I knew that I needed to develop a personal relationship with Christ and the Holy Spirit.
- I knew that I needed to dedicate myself to serving others, starting by serving the spiritual and emotional needs of my wife and family.
- Conclusively, I knew that I needed more than just a few tweaks to reach the depth of change the situation required—I needed a complete transformation.

Luckily, I was now beginning to understand what had been missing in my life and marriage, though I had few ideas where to start. The life I had been leading was not connected and it was not spiritually based. Christ was not at the center of my life or my marriage—only *I* was at the center, which left me feeling alone and lost. At that moment I knew it was time to fill the void and bring myself into alignment with God's purpose for me here on earth.

Because my whole life and being up until then had been predicated on my career, I was completely focused on matters of the flesh and of the world. Yet in my broken state, I became committed to be ready for change. Change is what happened.

The Lord came to me and spoke to me. He said that if I would allow Him into my heart, it would transform every aspect of my life. It would turn the equation around;

rather than my world being driven by my own wants and needs, I would begin serving the needs of the LORD and of others. It became my goal to become the spiritual leader of my family. With an open heart and a blossoming renewal of faith, I accepted this responsibility to grow.

Once the Holy Spirit came alive within me, how I began to change. The perception that others had of me also began to change. What others began to see in me was the Fruit of the Spirit, and not the works of the flesh. *The Fruit of the Spirit are those aspects of a deeper spiritual character that the bearer shares with those around him or her.* These points of character are like the fruit that grows from a tree that is strongly rooted. Thus, upon my spiritual growth taking root, the branches of my life were now beginning to blossom. This was a pivotal moment, a cause for celebration. It became a life-changing transformation, as I now live my life on a mission to share abundant spiritual fruit.

The Apostle Paul compared the fruit of the Spirit to the works of the flesh in Galatians 5:19–26:

> Now the works of the flesh are obvious: immorality, impurity, licentiousness, idolatry, sorcery, hatreds, rivalry, jealousy, outbursts of fury, acts of selfishness, dissensions, factions, occasions of envy, drinking bouts, orgies, and the like. I warn you, as I warned you before, that those who do such things will not inherit the kingdom of God. In contrast, the fruit of the Spirit is love, joy, peace, patience, kindness, generosity, faithfulness, gentleness, self-control. Against such there is no law. Now those who belong to Christ (Jesus) have crucified their flesh with its

> passions and desires. If we live in the Spirit, let us also follow the Spirit. Let us not be conceited, provoking one another, envious of one another.

There are three key messages that Paul offers in this critical passage. The first is that apart from the Spirit, we are slaves to our flesh, unable to break free from the baser-level qualities of our humanity's sinfulness. In this state we are incapable of attaining what the Lord has envisioned for us. The second message is that for our flesh to be transformed, we must allow the Holy Spirit into our hearts and lives to be our spiritual guide. Only then will others begin to recognize the fruit of the Spirit in us more than they would see the works of the flesh. The third key message is that this fruit is universally recognized as good and positive aspects of character and that "against such, there is no law."

Living in the Spirit is about asking the Lord for the faith and trust to focus our lives and marriages upon Christ. And it is through this commitment that we will become transformed. As the Holy Spirit becomes present, we begin taking on the characteristics of Christ. Welcoming the Holy Spirit into our hearts and trusting in His power, it will work to change us into more Christ-like versions of ourselves. Over time, as we further our relationship with Christ and trust in our transformation, these changes will become inherent to our character. The degree and shape to which the fruit manifests will be unique to each one of us.

The fruit of the Spirit will be present in all our actions and in our relationships. Having decided to follow Christ, decided to live according to His teachings, and having asked to be full of His Spirit, the fruit is what people will see. Just as smoke denotes fire, so does the fruit represent the workings of the Holy Spirit in the individual and in relationships.

Paul's list of the fruit of the Spirit and the works of the flesh to the Galatians outlines what qualities and characteristics our lives should represent and should not represent.

Fruit of the Spirit	Works of the Flesh
• *Love* • *Joy* • *Peace* • *Patience* • *Kindness* • *Generosity* • *Faithfulness* • *Gentleness* • *Self-Control*	• *Immorality* • *Impurity* • *Licentiousness* • *Idolatry* • *Sorcery* • *Hatreds* • *Rivalry* • *Jealousy* • *Outburst of Fury* • *Acts of Selfishness* • *Dissensions* • *Factions* • *Occasions of Envy* • *Drinking Bouts* • *Orgies* • *Conceit* • *Provocations* • *Envy*

Some claim that certain "of the flesh" characteristics may just be within someone's nature and that there is very little that can be done to change that. However, while it may be true that the potential for the works of flesh lies in each of us, it is only when we are devoid of the Holy Spirit that any of those negative characteristics take root. With the presence of the Spirit, none of the works of flesh can manifest in the character of the transformed person.

As an example, my wife once told me that generosity was something one had to be born with. I reminded her that generosity was a fruit of the Spirit, putting myself up as proof. She and everyone who knew me were well aware that I was born tight, stingy, and cheap. I had to be transformed to begin expressing a spirit of giving and generosity. This was only because I learned to allow the Spirit to work in me and lead me. I certainly wasn't born that way.

Another example that I can personally attest to is joyfulness. Once upon a time, I was not a very joyful or pleasant person to be around. In fact, because of my joyless demeanor, my wife saw little proof in our relationship that I even loved her. As I've shared in this book, it took a conscious decision by me to put Christ at the center of my life and to let the Holy Spirit be my guide. To make a personal metamorphosis, Paul instructs us in Ephesians 4:22–24:

> That you should put away the old self of your former way of life, corrupted through deceitful desires, and be renewed in the spirit of your minds, and put on the new self, created in God's way in righteousness and holiness of truth.

I needed to completely transform. And in so doing, I went through a kind of "death" to my old selfish self so that I could be reborn and live a life of greater power and service to others. It was Basic Salvation 101.

Not only did I become joyful, I began to bring joy to others. I asked God to help me transform my home to be a joyful place to live. I asked God to help me bring joy to others. Living a life of joy and bringing joy to others is a great way to live. When you allow the Holy Spirit to bring joy into your life, the joy comes from inside of you. You are not looking for your joy to come from others. You become a source of joy. The concept of "bringing home the joy" will be explored further in Chapter Eight: A Great Marriage Is Life Changing.

WHO'S IN CONTROL?

If you are bearing some (or even none) of the fruit, then who or what are you following? Have you ever gone through periods in life where you've thought, "I really don't need God's help right now; I'm doing great and can handle things just fine"? In 1 Thessalonians 5:19, Paul warns us against this kind of humanistic thinking when he says, "Do not quench the Spirit."

God has given us the free will to make many decisions in how we are to live our lives. However, who is in control, you or the Holy Spirit? If you want to live and follow in the Spirit, share the fruit of the Spirit, and help others to walk in the Spirit, it must come from God. There can only be one in charge. In John 3:30–31, John the Baptist speaks directly to this hierarchy:

> "He must increase; I must decrease." The one who comes from above is above all. The one who is of the

earth is earthly and speaks of earthly things. But the one who comes from heaven (is above all).

In the first few years of my marriage I would often walk in the door in the evening and begin complaining about how "I've had a hard day; leave me alone; let me relax; I can't talk right now." That was not the Spirit; it was my flesh pressing me to escape from dealing with my core issues. In those moments I had decided that I was too busy for God, didn't need His help, and that I was just going to be me.

Giving control over to the will of the Holy Spirit has been the most important, meaningful, and liberating decision I've made in my life. Following Christ as my model has been the "truth" spoken of in John 8:31–32:

> Jesus then said to those Jews who believed in him, "If you remain in my word, you will truly be my disciples, and you will know the truth, and the truth will set you free."

I want the people in my life to see Christ. I don't want them to see me in the flesh. I want them to see me in the Spirit. Thus, I am always asking myself, "Am I being led by the Spirit or have *I* taken over? Who am I letting guide me at this moment?" My wife says that after I began living the Spirit, when I would come home, there would be joy. Believe me, this was not the "human me"—I was coming home in the Spirit. I would pray, talk with God, and basically do whatever it took so that what my family saw when I came home was the fruit of the Spirit. It really didn't matter how hard my day might have been or whatever I might have been struggling with at the time; I decided to not let concerns of the flesh control me. When I walked in the house, I wanted my family to see me as a man who has been called by God.

Thus, the lesson I eventually learned was that no matter how anxious, frustrated, worried, or confused I might have felt, before I arrived home and unloaded my burdens on my spouse and family, I needed to share them with God. *God, why did you let that happen today? What's going on?* I learned to give all my troubles over to God and trust that He was listening. Then as I walked through the door to my home, I had already made the decision to let the Holy Spirit guide me and let His fruit be the manifestations of the Spirit within me.

INSTANT FEEDBACK

I was amazed and delighted that once I'd made the decision to live in the Spirit, it seemed to bear fruit immediately. It became infectious with my wife and family reflecting back what I was projecting on them, like a mirror. What a terrific instant-feedback mechanism! Had I not been actually sharing the fruit of the Spirit by living the Spirit, it would have been clear by the reactions and interactions with my family. As the spiritual head of the family, I needed to lead by example by making the conscious decision to only share those characteristics and qualities described by Paul as "in the Spirit."

It became clear to me that to stay on track I would need my wife's feedback. Thus, I began asking Elaine to help me discern if my actions and words demonstrated good fruit. If my intentions were ever to seem contrary to the values of love or joy or peace or patience, she has full permission to correct me by letting me know. By giving my spouse the right to *adjust* me, I am helping myself to grow. Just being open to her feedback has proven a major success for me, bringing new life to my marriage and helping me to focus on living a more Christ-like life. Elaine is my special gift from God. I give her thanks and tremendous credit for her loving heart and helpful hand in our journey toward a Christ-centered marriage.

My spouse is a gift to me from God. Your spouse is a gift to you from God. In the sacrament of marriage, God gave us a grace to become one. Led by the Holy Spirit, I asked my spouse to help me follow Jesus. I gave her the right to help and correct me. What a joy to see the Holy Spirit work through my spouse to help me to grow with the Lord.

If any of us were operating in the flesh, how would we react to our spouse's suggestions? We would probably respond with anger. The flesh defiantly tries to defend itself, its actions, and its motivations. Unless we want to live in the Spirit, we are not going to be correctable or teachable, and it becomes very hard for others to help us. It's interesting to note that all those behaviors that make us difficult to deal with and live with come from the flesh. And when we operate from the flesh, we are not open to change. And when not open to change, we become stuck in a way of living that expends tremendous energy defending itself. What a waste of our personal resources!

Each of us has family and friends who would love to see us living and sharing the fruit of the Holy Spirit. They are the best allies in our discernment of our Christ-like characteristics from those in the flesh. Paul tries to help us understand the spiritual way of living through his letter to the Galatians. However, the responsibility lies on us to be open to this new way of living and allow the spirit to transform us. Which once again ties back to the question of control: Are you letting the flesh or the Holy Spirit control your life?

THE LONG-TERM EFFECTS

When you begin to let the Holy Spirit take control, most aspects of your life will be transformed. Importantly, your relationships with family, friends, coworkers, and acquaintances will change. By deciding to follow Christ's teachings and begin living the fruit of the Spirit, you will see remarkable changes in how you perceive and interact with those around you. You will begin to see others more like our Holy Father sees them, as unique, special, and capable. Even those people who you envision to be your persecutors and your enemies—those who clearly may not be led by the Spirit—God created and loves. He wants you to love them too.

The issue is not, "If I'm really a Christian and living the fruit of the Spirit, why are others still treating me this way?" The issue should be, "I want to help them have a closer relationship with God, just as I am striving for, and thus I will let them see the Spirit in my actions." How I decide to live my life and treat others dictates the nature of my relationships.

In my thirty-plus years of working with couples and individuals becoming renewed in their faith, one of the central pieces of advice I've given has been to break from old patterns and decide to share only the fruit of the Spirit. Getting angry and reflecting back on others a mind-set of the flesh does not move anyone closer to God. Are any of the earthly and temporary squabbles really so important when compared to God's promise to you of eternal life? As Paul instructs in Ephesians 5:8–10:

> For you were once darkness, but now you are light in the Lord. Live as children of light, for light produces every kind of goodness and righteousness and truth. Try to learn what is pleasing to the Lord.

Understand that His goal for all of us is salvation from the evils and pettiness present in the world. To be children of God, it is critical that we help bring people to the Spirit. Living and sharing the fruit sows the best seeds for a successful harvest of happy and fulfilling relationships, thus bringing our personal transformation full circle.

THE TWO SHALL BECOME ONE

A SPIRITUAL UNION

Becoming one with our spouse means being willing to change, to focus on their needs, and to grow into more loving, Christ-like versions of ourselves. The closest thing we can experience on earth to becoming one with Christ is developing a great marriage, with two becoming one in spiritual union.

In Catholicism, there are seven sacraments. "Sacraments are outward signs of inward grace, instituted by Christ for our sanctification" (Catechismus Council, Trent., N.4, ex Saint Augustine, *De Catechizandis Rudibus*). Marriage is the seventh sacrament. However, unlike the other sacraments, it is a covenant; no other sacrament asks us to become one with another human. The other six sacraments involve varying conditions of spiritual commitment:

- *Baptism* is to become a child of god.
- *First Communion* is to seek and receive the body of Christ.

- *Confirmation* is to be willing to be transformed—with the help of the Holy Spirit—to follow Christ and to become a witness for others.
- *Reconciliation* is the asking for forgiveness of sins so you are cleansed back to your baptismal state.
- *Holy Orders* is saying that you want to serve in a deeper way, wanting to become one with Lord and one with the church.
- *Anointing of the Sick* is a combination of being cleansed of sin and being healed.

The vows recited during the marriage ceremony illustrate the significance of *two becoming one:*

> I take you to be my wife/husband;
> I promise to be true to you in good times and in bad,
> In sickness and in health;
> I will love you and honor you all the days of my life.

So it was God's intention from the beginning—and taught to us by Jesus—that when we come together as husband and wife, we remain together until death. As Mark 10: 6–9 states:

> But from the beginning of creation, "God made them male and female. For this reason a man shall leave his father and mother (and be joined to his wife), and the two shall become one flesh." So they are no longer two but one flesh. Therefore what God has joined together, no human being must separate.

In a Catholic wedding, the bride and groom come before God to receive the marriage sacrament witnessed by the minister, which is a priest or deacon. The minister and the couple's family and friends all participate in the ceremony to pray for the couple and to celebrate their special day. But most importantly, they are there to support the two as a couple from that day forward, throughout their married life. Preceding the wedding vows in the rite of marriage is the statement of intentions, whereby the minister asks the couple three questions:

- Have you come here freely and without reservation to give yourselves to each other in marriage?
- Will you honor each other as man and wife for the rest of your lives?
- Will you accept children lovingly from God and bring them up according to the law of Christ and His church?

The statement of intentions serves a twofold purpose: The first is to assure the good of the spouses and that both are capable of loving someone and being loved unconditionally and permanently. The second purpose is the transmission of life through procreation.

When a man and woman come together to become one in the Lord, they commit to do several things. They commit to each other: for better or worse; for richer or for poorer; in sickness and in health. Whenever I hear this, I am reminded of one couple who wanted to memorize their vows. I suggested that they repeat them after me, but they insisted. On the day of the wedding, the groom forgot a few words ("in sickness and in health"). After the wedding, the bride asked me if they were really indeed married because of the groom's omissions in the vows. I assured her they were married but also suggested that she do her best to not get sick.

Marriage success is more than just signing the marriage contract. I've been in business a long time and have worked on a great number of meaningful projects, but I confess that rarely has a contract brought me great joy. My marriage and commitment to my wife, however, has brought me almost unlimited happiness. It has been a wonderful journey.

LOVE ONE ANOTHER

Jesus commanded each of us to love one another. In John 15:12–13, he teaches, "This is my commandment: love one another as I love you. No one has greater love than this, to lay down one's life for one's friends."

Therefore, love is not a feeling. To love is a decision—a decision both a man and woman make together. Following Christ is an individual's decision, though. If you plan on spending eternity with God, preparing yourself should be your top priority. Your second priority is your relationship with your spouse—becoming one with them.

God has given you your spouse to help you learn how to become one with Him. He gave your spouse to you to be your best friend, to teach you how to love, to teach you how to forgive, to teach you how to change and to grow, and to come to know the nature of God's love for you. God is not the one who needs to change. If we wish to be one with Him, it is us who should transform. God is going to help all along the way, if we ask Him and are then prepared to act. Jesus prayed in John 17:20–21:

> I pray not only for them, but also for those who will believe in me through their word, so that they may all be one, as you, Father, are in me and I in you, that they also may be in us, that the world may believe that you sent me.

As you grow in your relationship with God, He will teach you to show love to those who share your life. Learning how to unconditionally love is a process and the result of experiences, prayer, decisions, instruction, and insight. It is not earned without some effort.

Some may believe that the model established by their parents' marriage should automatically apply regardless of whether their parents had a great marriage or not. Some women envision a Cinderella-style fairytale, living happily ever after and walking hand in hand with her Prince Charming. Some men rarely seem motivated in setting a lifetime goal of being the ever-charming prince. Today, both men and women may believe that once the honeymoon comes to an end, it's time to get back into their regular patterns of living and focusing on career ambition and material goals. This was my initial model for marriage.

As mentioned, Elaine and I have been happily married for over thirty-eight years, and we recently celebrated our forty-seventh anniversary. While we may disagree on how many of those early years were even mediocre, we have since learned what it means to be happily married. And we definitely agree that the years we define as *great* were a result of our marriage being centered upon Christ.

SO WHY ISN'T EVERYONE HAVING A GREAT MARRIAGE?

Recall that approximately 50 percent of all new marriages end in divorce. In terms of statistical probability, you are just as likely to win in a coin toss as to win at marriage. Of course, the flipside of this means 50 percent of marriages actually do survive until death do they part. There was a popular movie many years ago called *The Italian Divorce,* which showcased a morbidly creative approach to dealing with an unhappy marriage. Its premise was that because the unhappily married wife could not get a divorce, she plotted to kill her husband. Most assuredly, that was *not* what God intended with "until death do us part."

Yet merely staying together does not necessarily mean that the union is a great success either. Couples that do stay together can generally be put into three categories:

- Approximately 40 *percent stay together* because of the commitment they have made—to their spouse, their children, or even their possessions—but would not describe their marriage as great or even good. These marriages are characterized by equal numbers of good times and bad times. Spouses in this category are simply just committed. It is important to note, however, that you do not have to stay in an abusive relationship.

- Approximately 40 *percent stay together* because they have learned to live together but have plenty of ups and downs in their marriage. Though these marriages are characterized by more good times than bad times, spouses in this category may not even know that great marriages can and do exist.
- What remains is the approximately 20 *percent of couples* that survive and figure out how to have a great marriage. Spouses in these relationships consistently have good times. They have become more than just partners—*they are becoming one.*

Remaining together can be difficult, particularly these days. Laws allowing divorce make it easy and impersonal to break the marriage union, with little negative stigma being tied to divorce in our culture. Society now accepts that people will leave their marriage if they are not happy. Many people considered successful—high-profile stars, business leaders, and politicians—approach marriage as if it should be easy and enjoyable. Many do not spend sufficient time working on their marriages. Instead, they believe that their marriage should be something that "works" for them. Then when married life proves to be no easy task, rather than putting in the time and effort to seek out the causes of the problems and work through solutions, they simply decide to move on.

For the many marriages that do end in divorce, many factors can contribute to the break up. As will be evident in our own testimony, my wife and I have battled and lived through several of these challenges. Let's first address some of the major ones, all stemming from poor communication:

1. Addictions and distractions
2. "Judgmentalism"
3. Unwillingness to change
4. Loss of faith in marriage

An understanding of some of the general causes and symptoms of these will be helpful in addressing them as challenges that can be overcome. They are not insurmountable obstacles. The Lord has given each of us the free will to determine our own path in choosing how we respond to our personal struggles. As our beacon, He sent us His Son, Jesus, to save us and His Holy Spirit to guide us. Through them, committed couples can learn to better communicate and solve any issue.

Addictions and Distractions

Life in today's world offers an unending parade of distractions and addictions. Career, personal priorities, and insignificant diversions can take precedence over one's focus on building a successful marriage. Addictions can also take many forms, playing upon our likes and dislikes, as well as our strengths and weaknesses. My own addictions to working and making money serve as a perfect example for how these things can damage your relationships with those people you care about.

Essentially, anything that can be done in excess has the potential to become an addiction or distraction, such as working, materialism, eating, drinking, drugs, gambling, watching TV, sex, pornography, golfing, making/spending money, education, etc. Situations such as these can result in compulsive and obsessive behavior that is out of touch with reality. As a consequence, addiction to anything carries with it the dangerous potential of distracting you from your marriage priorities and coming between you and your spouse and God. Addictions can easily take over the number one priority position. In Romans 7:18–19, Paul shares:

> For I know that good does not dwell in me, that is, in my flesh. The willing is ready at hand, but doing the good is not. For I do not do the good I want, but I do the evil I do not want.

Ironically, some Christian married couples let their participation in church distract them from working on improving their marriage. As a deacon for over thirty years, this is something to which I too have confessed being guilty. Though involvement in the church is important, it must be taken in moderation and balanced with the other key activities of one's life. Couples must determine the appropriate level of participation for their family. I've led counseling sessions where one spouse is an active participant in the church and the other spouse is the opposite and rarely participates. The active spouse then justifies their actions and the commitment they have to their faith as doing "God's work," believing they are doing the right thing by putting God first in their life. However, God is not the one telling them to do the extreme level of ministering and church activity. Rather, they have talked themselves into believing that they are doing it all for God, which ironically results in taking too much time away from their spouse and family.

Many point to the busyness of their lives causing this reshuffling and confusion of priorities. This defense does not hold up; poorly assessed priorities in life are not a byproduct of being busy or having many things to do. Self-centered partners are those who are more focused on themselves and their various distractions and addictions in life than on their most important relationships. The relationship with their spouse becomes low on the priority list—or perhaps not even ranking on the priority list. In this situation the couple is not living as one. They are not living according to the "one flesh" commandment in Matthew's Gospel. As our spiritual father, God must be our first priority. However, to focus our lives here on earth, He wishes our second priority to be our spouses.

In working with couples, one common theme I've learned is that if Christ is not at the center of the lives of the husband and/or wife, something else will be their focus. For me it was work and money; with others it may be drugs, alcohol, sex, materialism, education, work, etc. The list of false gods can go on and on. It could be something considered sinful, or it could be a thing perceived as good, such as work or education. But if these things become our God, our main focuses, then they distract us from what should be our focus: being children of God and following Jesus.

"Judgmentalism"

Another major challenge is "judgmentalism," as some troubled marriages suffer from one or both spouses placing undue and unwanted criticism on their partner. Rather than working together to overcome the obstacles in their marriage, judgmental spouses attempt to justify divorce by focusing on the flaws in their spouse. Once having convinced themselves they deserve a divorce, they often seek out the company of other divorcees to find justification to their actions.

Spouses passing judgment on each other has proven to be the undoing of many well-intended marriages. Rather than working through their obstacles together with the help of a pastor or marriage professional, these troubled couples justify their unhappiness by placing the blame on their partner. They build their case that the root of the marriage problems is their spouse's fault. Once they feel justified in seeking divorce, the judging spouse will show little interest in talking to anyone about the issues in their marriage or listening to any solutions to their problems. That includes opening up and hearing wisdom from God. The New Testament is very clear on the topic of judging others, as evident in Romans 2:1: "Therefore, you are without excuse, every one of you who passes judgment. For by the standard by which you judge another you condemn yourself, since you, the judge, do the very same things."

Spouses who are in these relationships just want out. In addition to judging their partner, they most likely also have been keeping score, and often without their spouse even knowing it! In Matthew 7:2, Jesus teaches us the long-term penalty of judging others: "For as you judge, so will you be judged, and the measure with which you measure will be measured out to you."

Nowhere in the marriage vows does it say that when a man and woman become husband and wife it is a spouse's job to judge the other. Unfortunately, that is how most of us live—believing that by being bonded in marriage God has anointed us to be our spouse's most vocal critic. Spouses in such marriages think, as I did, *If my spouse would just change…* However, true change in the relationship does not come from spouses judging one another. Couples can only become one by allowing God, through prayer, to help them both to change. The intention of the wedding vows is to let God bestow His grace on your marriage and help each of you through each other. Our goal should be to be more like Christ.

Resistance to Change

A third challenge to having a great marriage is when one or both partners approach the relationship with a "what's in it for me?" attitude. This usually creates an expectation that it is one partner's responsibility to make the other partner happy. The result is that one or both spouses then become resistant to personal change.

Some married individuals may have a limited understanding of what it actually means to be a good spouse. I have worked with couples in the past where one or both spouses complain that they are giving more than their fair share of a fifty-fifty marriage. The point I try to make to them is that love or marriage is not a fifty-fifty proposition.

As an exercise, I'll start by separating them, and I'll first ask the husband, "If marriage is fifty-fifty, how are you doing?"

The typical response is, "I am giving eighty, and she is giving twenty."

Then I'll go talk to the wife. "If marriage is fifty-fifty, how are you doing?"

She may tell me, "I am giving eighty, and he is giving twenty."

I'll then call them together and tell them that it was actually a trick question, as a marriage is not fifty-fifty. *Marriage requires a* 100 *percent giving commitment.*

Think about it: have you ever committed to anything 50 percent and done it well? I have found that partial commitments are merely intentions which the person lacks the courage to follow through. The reason the percentage question is tricky is because each of these spouses actually believes that they are the one doing most of the work; they believe their spouse needs to change more than they themselves need to change.

I can speak to this with firsthand experience. Remember, once upon a time my favorite prayer was, "Lord, change my wife." From the initial results of that prayer, I assumed that either God had not heard me or that perhaps He just did not answer prayers.

Eventually, though, after spending many hours studying Jesus' Sermon on the Mount, I began to understand Matthew 7:3, when Jesus asks, "Why do you notice the splinter in your brother's eye, but do not perceive the wooden beam in your own eye?"

Once I began taking personal responsibility for my own change and attitude by asking God to change me, I never had to pray the "Lord, change my wife" prayer again.

Your spouse should be your best friend. Unfortunately, some couples find that quickly rededicating themselves to their marriage or their friendship is difficult.

Many unhappy spouses go through years of convincing themselves that they deserve a divorce, creating a mind-set that their spouse is not going to change. These determined people usually do not like speaking to a person in the church because of what they know they will hear. The Catholic marriage counselor will most likely advise them that they should not immediately pursue a divorce until after attempting to work through the issues.

The Catholic Church puts tremendous prayer and thought into keeping marriages together—both before and after the actual marriage ceremony. Catholics believe that when the bride and the groom stand in church before God and repeat their vows, He bestows grace upon them. He blesses them with the opportunity of being with their best friend for life.

If you want to begin changing your marriage today, *recognize that your spouse is a gift from God and treat them as such.* Regardless of how perfect or imperfect the relationship is, and assuming you are not in an abusive relationship, be grateful for your marriage and thank God for your spouse. The best way to show this is by making your spouse the top priority in your life, second only to your relationship with God. We'll continue to explore this approach throughout the book.

Loss of Faith in Marriage

When Jesus was asked about the appropriateness of divorce, in Matthew 19:5–6, He responded by saying:

> For this reason a man shall leave his father and mother and be joined to his wife, and the two shall become one flesh. So they are no longer two, but one flesh. Therefore, what God has joined together, no human being must separate.

Although this is a very popular scripture for use in weddings, there is often a lack of understanding what the concept of two becoming one actually means. It refers to the bond of faith in the union between the bride and groom.

When faith in the sacrament is missing, husbands and wives shut themselves off from the grace of God helping them work through the challenges of marriage. Because they no longer believe God is speaking to them through their spouses, they, in turn, cease listening. And as such, they no longer allow the Holy Spirit to work through their spouse to help them live better lives. Hebrews 11:1 reiterates the importance of faith: "Faith is the realization of what is hoped for and evidence of things not seen."

Having faith in your daily married lives is critical. In situations where the marriage ends in divorce, the couple has lost faith. As 2 Corinthians 5:7 states, "For we walk by faith, not by sight."

Marriages that end in divorce are often due to one or both of the spouses putting focus on the material world, walking by sight rather than by faith. Hebrews 11:6 says, "But without faith it is impossible to please Him, for anyone who approaches God must believe that He exists and that He rewards those who seek him."

A married couple should believe that having a successful marriage is possible, if they trust their marriage to God. Likewise, in relationships where one partner expects the other to make them happy and address only their needs or problems, the patience and commitment to each other that comes with faith is missing.

LIVING IN THE HOLY SPIRIT

Jesus promised that if you follow Him, it will change your life in more powerful and meaningful ways than you can imagine—and it will. Choosing to change your life by working to understand the gospel and to live in the Holy Spirit will lead you down the right path—the path to becoming one with the LORD. John 8:31–32 tells us, "Jesus then said to those who believed in Him, If you remain in My word, you will truly be My disciples and you will know the truth, and the truth will set you free."

To understand the real meaning of what Jesus calls "the truth," you must live according to the wisdom of His words and life. One of your greatest opportunities to do this will be in developing and growing your relationship with your spouse. It is the commitment of a husband and wife to serve each other through their marriage that most closely resembles Christ's love for His church. Ephesians 5:25 states, "Husbands, love your wives, even as Christ loved the church and handed himself over for her."

Jesus was willing to lay down His life for the good of His church and followers. So should a committed husband or wife be willing to lay down their own individual needs for the one they have committed to for life.

Successful Christian marriages don't just happen overnight or by magic. *They are built by both spouses living each of these qualities in their relationship day in and day out.* Living in this way is how we put Jesus at the center of our marriage.

The dynamics of modern culture and changing societal values have brought an enormous amount of focus to the self—"what is in it for me?" This approach has proven to be a dismal failure at providing any real joy or happiness for the individual or, not to mention, for those hopelessly in orbit around them. The most joyful people do not live their lives with this "me first" attitude. Rather than needing to have the best of everything, they make the most out of everything they have. We should all learn to love as Christ loved, to let go of the need for loving material things, and to compassionately love others and cherish our personal relationships. The great marriage that you and your spouse deserve will be built upon this foundation.

LIVING A BALANCED LIFE

THE FISHES ASSESSMENT

One of the things I ask married couples is how satisfied they are with their lives. Some consider this a very difficult question to answer. Rather than analyze the specific issues and aspects, some fall back on the law of averages and give the standard "I'm satisfied" answer. Upon further discussion, they usually are able to cite a few areas of their lives where they are pleased with where they are - and a few areas not so much. God wants us to be satisfied with all aspects of our lives. In attaining satisfaction and balance, an important first step is assessing where we are now and where we want to be.

The life-satisfaction/life-balance assessment exercise I lead couples in is a simple one called *FISHES*. This is an acronym for six high-priority areas of focus in leading a balanced life: Family, Intellect, Social Life, Health, Economic, and Spiritual. The general categories in FISHES are six of the most common, and on an individual basis, other categories may exist. Each person should do the exercise using the top six priorities they have set for themselves. In addition to employing this assessment when working with married couples, I also use it when working with engaged couples, dating couples, and singles seeking spiritual direction.

This is an effective activity for self-analysis and for generating feedback. The exercise gives you and your spouse, fiancé(e), or boyfriend/girlfriend an opportunity to assess how satisfied you are in the most important areas of your lives. For categories that score low, you can then discuss things you can do differently to improve them. Finding balance and consistency should be your overall objective. FISHES is a "big picture," straightforward exercise meant to help you assess your total life.

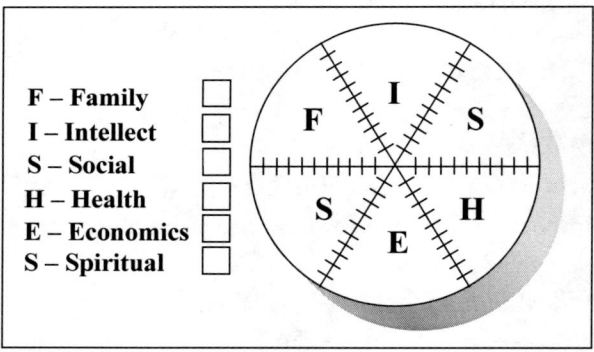

The steps for FISHES are:

1. You and your spouse, fiancé(e), girlfriend/boyfriend or significant other should rate your current level of life satisfaction in each of the FISHES areas using

a ten-point scale, with one being the lowest and ten representing the highest. Chart your levels on the FISHES circle by placing a dot at the appropriate mark. Then connect the dots between the axes. How balanced does your FISHES chart look? Are there any areas that are particularly strong or any that seem deficient?

2. The next step is to go back around the circle again; this time, however, indicate what you would like your levels of life satisfaction to be in each area.

3. Finally, add up and compare the scores of your current life satisfaction with your desired life satisfaction. What actions or things would you need to do differently to bring your current scores into alignment with your desired scores?

4. Share and compare charts with your spouse. How similar or dissimilar are your scores? If not the FISHES categories, do you and your spouse have other categories you've set as priorities? Discuss ways in which both can support each other's plans for improvement.

THE FISHES QUESTIONNAIRE

Asking yourself poignant "how am I doing?" questions can help you re-explore your expectations and determine your current level of life satisfaction and balance in each of the FISHES areas. This section offers several questions that will ask you to look at your actions—what you are actually living and doing—and then honestly reflect on where you currently are, where you once were, and where you would like to be. You should flag those questions that challenge you or offer hope, then prioritize which ones you would like to focus on and give them disciplined attention. Because your perspectives will probably change over time, you might find value in recording your answers in a personal journal. Comparing perspectives from different points in time can show you those areas where you've made progress and those that may require more motivation or focus.

Family

What a challenge, being a good spouse, a parent, a son, or a daughter—being in a family! The demands of normal daily family life can leave one feeling unappreciated and overburdened. Do not be dismayed. As it says in Philippians 4:19: "My God will fully supply whatever you need, in accord with his glorious riches in Christ Jesus." And Jesus' commandment to us in John 15:12–13 was to love: "This is my commandment: love one another as I love you. No one has greater love than this, to lay down one's life for one's friends." According to this commandment, love is not a feeling—rather, love is a decision. When the decision is made to love, we also make the decision to lay down our life for our spouse and our family—meaning daily living and praising God for your life and for your spouse and family.

Here are some questions you may ask yourself about your family life:

1. In what ways do you put your family's needs above your own?
2. Are you respectful of one another, even when criticized or in a disagreement?
3. Do you regularly share meals together?
4. With your spouse and as a family, do you make it a practice to engage in meaningful conversations?
5. How are you a good example for others?
6. How often do you pray together?
7. How often do you play together?
8. Do you encourage a family environment that is relaxed, spontaneous, and flexible
9. Do you have an intimate, loving, and healthy sex life with your spouse?
10. Do you say, "I love you," often and show it?
11. Are you forgiving?
12. Are you patient?
13. Are you instructive?
14. Are you thoughtful?
15. Do you regularly ask yourself what it would be like to be married to you?
16. Have you and your spouse established a framework of family rules?
17. Do you offer praise and recognition for accomplishment?

18. Do you encourage verbal communications between family members that is frequent, diverse, open, and honest?
19. Do you share family stories and history?
20. How often do you schedule time for your family?
21. Are you careful to not over-schedule children's activity time?
22. What family traditions or rituals have you established?
23. Do you compliment often and praise good behavior among your family members?
24. Does each of your family members, including yourself, have individual responsibilities, and are they held accountable for them?
25. How do you outwardly express your love?
26. Do you understand the true biblical meaning of love?
27. Do you control the quality and quantity of TV watched in your home?
28. Do you keep a clean and tidy home?
29. Do you create an energetic environment for your family and demonstrate a positive attitude?

Intellect

Less than 2 percent of people pursue any type of educational or intellectual objective after they have received their high school or college diploma. Additionally, only 2 percent of Catholics go on retreats. Think about it: if you would like to be in the top 10 percent of all marriages, consider what you would do to improve yourself intellectually—be it learning a new skill, attending classes, or reading more books, including the Bible.

Some questions you can ask yourself:

1. Have you tried meditation techniques for prayer and relaxation?
2. If you have attained your formal education goals, are you continuing to pursue new, informal ones that tap your passion or pique your interest?
3. Do you look for learning experiences in everyday life, as well as in new activities, travel, etc.?
4. Are you organized, do you set priorities, and do you manage your time well?
5. When faced with decisions or problems, do you think of multiple solutions, as well as their results or consequences?
6. Do you discuss your ideas with others?
7. Do you practice keeping an open mind?
8. Do you challenge yourself to exceed the boundaries of your comfort zone?
9. Have you learned to control worry and anxiety?
10. Are you developing your writing and speaking skills?
11. Do you make it a point to read/watch/listen to motivational materials on a regular basis?

12. Do you read the Bible, participate in Bible study, and go on retreats?
13. Do you make a habit of taking courses and learning new skills?
14. Are you inquisitive and ask questions?
15. Do you do word searches and immediately look up definitions to words you don't know?
16. Do you have an active reading/learning program to develop or further your knowledge, skills, interests, and awareness?
17. Are you constantly working on improving your memory using such tools as association, imagination, and location?
18. Have you identified and focused on your best learning style, be it sight (print) or sound (audio) or perhaps even touch, smell, or taste or a combination of these?
19. Are emotional issues holding you back from pursuing intellectual issues? Learning requires focus.
20. Do you use available techniques for improving your IQ?
21. Have you joined a book club?
22. Do you use puzzles and other mental exercises to challenge your intellect?
23. Do you keep an idea journal?
24. Do you discriminately utilize the Internet to research and learn?

25. Do you periodically utilize your learned real math skills rather than just depending on electronic devices to solve computations?
26. Are you well read on a horizon of different subjects?
27. Have you learned to speed read?
28. Have you learned one or more foreign languages?
29. Do you try focusing rather than multitasking?
30. Do you plan out projects in advance?
31. Are your behaviors and habits predictable, or do you "shake things up" from time to time?
32. When traveling, do you learn about the area, its history, economy, etc.?

Social Life

When looking at your social goals and assessing whether you are happy with your social life, ask yourself just how active you really are in engaging others socially. Some areas you might consider:

1. Are you involved in church, sports, dinner, your family, your neighborhood, playing cards, hobbies, and civic, career, or other social groups?
2. Do you smile and make eye contact when talking with others?
3. Are you reliable? Can you be counted on?
4. Are you learning to use humor more often?

5. Do you dress well and have good personal hygiene and grooming habits?
6. Do you help others without expecting a "thank you" or recognition?
7. Are you forgiving?
8. Do you volunteer in worthwhile community service activities and projects?
9. Do you let your social life just happen, or do you proactively plan social events?
10. Do you date your spouse, fiancé(e), or girlfriend/boyfriend?
11. Do you make friendly conversation with people you don't know?
12. When talking with others, do you show a genuine interest in them?
13. Do you really listen to what others are saying?
14. After meeting someone you would like to know better, do you suggest a subsequent get-together?
15. Do you remember other people's names, birthdays, anniversaries, and other momentous events?
16. Do you take yourself too seriously?
17. Are you cynical?
18. Do you bully others?
19. Are you aware of and do you practice proper social etiquette?

20. Do you exude confidence in your speech and behavior?
21. Are you self-reliant or dependent on others?
22. Do you admit your mistakes?
23. Are you manipulative?
24. Are you controlling?
25. How often do you give a gift to someone for no particular reason other than love and friendship?
26. Do you ask for what you need from others?
27. Are you flexible in your habits and behavior?
28. Are you truthful?
29. Are you patient?
30. Have you eliminated negative people and circumstances from your life, if possible?

Health

I once read a book that said that the main reason that women live longer than men is because women go to the doctor. Having talked with many couples on how they prioritize good health practices, I would tend to agree. A few years ago, I heard the head of the Methodist Hospital in Houston speak to a group about life choices. He said that most hospitalized people below the age of fifty are there because of life choices, such as smoking or accidents. After fifty, however, is when your body starts making choices for you. Whether its stubbornness or machismo, men tend to wait until something hurts before they see a doctor. The problem with waiting until something hurts when you are over fifty is that by that age, it's usually too late for easy treatments.

I have taken a physical every year since my thirties, and I have three diseases (high blood pressure, low thyroid, and prostate cancer) that would kill me if I didn't follow my simple medication treatments. I recently had a physical and asked my doctor, "What is the hardest thing you have to deal with in your patients?"

He said, "Even when they come in, they don't take the medication I prescribe them. Then when they come back in, their conditions are more advanced." I hope to continue being one of his easy patients.

When you grow together as one in the LORD, you and your spouse will experience how following Jesus is a healthy way to live. Honesty, kindness, commitment, moderation, thoughtfulness, duty, sharing love, etc., all offer health benefits. Some additional thoughts for consideration:

1. Is your weight within the medically recommended range for your body type?
2. Do you eat a balanced diet?
3. How do you feel about yourself when you look at your body in the mirror?
4. Do you get periodic medical screening exams as recommended for your age?
5. Are you following the prescribed treatment for any health conditions you might have?

6. Do you exercise regularly?
7. Do you practice stress relief techniques?
8. Do you drink alcohol too much or too often?
9. Are you addicted to any kind of drugs, whether prescribed or not?
10. Do you have an active prayer life (which research shows improves your health)?
11. Do you practice positive affirmations to love yourself?
12. Do you know God loves you?
13. Do you appreciate the present as the perfect time, or do you engage in longing for the past and dreaming of the future?
14. Are you attuned to your instincts, and do you trust them?
15. Do you take short power naps during the day?
16. Do you maintain good personal hygiene?
17. Do you smoke?
18. Do you practice deep breathing to infuse your lungs and brain with oxygen?
19. Do you start the day with a good breakfast?

Economics

The happiest couples are the ones that learn to live with what they have and stay within a budget. This goes counter to the "more is better" mentality predominant in a consumption-driven culture. Being successful with money is not about how much you have but what you do with what you have. I advise people to take a simple approach to economics—spend less than you make. If you want financial freedom and the ability to help others, spend 20 percent less than you make. Handling economics this way will allow you to comfortably manage most of the financial emergencies that may crop up, and you will hopefully have a little money left over to lend or give to your relatives or friends in need. Remember, however, to consider loans to family and friends as gifts and to not expect repayment. It's also important that spouses communicate frequently about finances and that financial decisions are shared. Some areas you might consider:

1. Do you set annual financial goals?
2. Do you spend less than you make?
3. Do you have a savings/investment/retirement plan that you follow?
4. Do you save on an automatic, planned basis?
5. Do you routinely track and monitor your bank and credit card accounts?
6. Do you give to your church and give to charity?
7. Do you have a last will and testament?
8. Do you involve your family in financial discussions?
9. Do you and your spouse make joint financial decisions?

10. Do you have a yearly and monthly budget and track it?
11. Do you regularly determine your net worth and measure it from year-to-year?
12. Are you satisfied that your savings will be sufficient for your children's college and your retirement?
13. Do you have an emergency fund to cover unforeseen expenses?
14. Are you invested across several asset classes to reduce risk?
15. Do you have an orderly system for keeping records?
16. Are you maximizing your retirement contributions?
17. Do you ask for discounts?
18. Do you use coupons cost effectively?
19. Do you comparison shop?
20. Do you have a durable universal power of attorney?
21. Do you have a durable medical power of attorney?
22. If you have credit cards, do you use them wisely?
23. Do you monitor your credit card report and score?
24. Is your debt manageable, or, better yet, are you out of debt?
25. Do you have adequate life, health, disability, home, and auto insurance?
26. Do you gamble?

27. Do you allow some time to think before making a purchasing decision?
28. Are you resentful of relatives or friends who may have borrowed money from you?

Spirituality

A close faith relationship with Jesus Christ, our Lord and Savior, is as good as it gets. No other relationship holds the peace and promise of this special bond as that between God and his children. Jesus taught us that love and forgiveness were the key elements to sharing life with Him. With God-centered inner peace, the Holy Spirit enters our lives and provides the fruits of the Spirit that we all crave. Some questions to ask yourself about your spiritual development:

1. Is God your number one priority?
2. Is your spouse your number two priority?
3. Are you in love with Jesus?
4. What is your life purpose?
5. What is your eternal purpose?
6. Do you actively and obediently practice your Christian faith?
7. If Catholic, do you regularly confess your sins in the sacrament of reconciliation?
8. Do you regularly receive the sacrament of Holy Communion and with a thankful adoring heart?

9. Do you read and study the Bible for love of God?
10. Do you practice the great commandment of love as described by Jesus?
11. Do you regularly and often thank God for his many blessings?
12. Do you pray or meditate regularly?
13. Is the fruit of the Spirit visible in your life?
14. Do you practice random acts of kindness?
15. Do you give freely and without expecting anything in return?
16. Do you attend Bible study?
17. Do you attend religious retreats?
18. Do you measure success by worldly standards or by godly Christian standards?
19. Do you abide by the Ten Commandments?
20. Do you keep a daily spiritual journal?
21. Are you making an effort to listen to the Holy Spirit in times when you feel you need guidance?
22. Are you a good Christian example?
23. Are you forgiving?
24. Do you ask for forgiveness?
25. Are you positive?
26. How do you measure success in life?

27. If unsatisfied with your current spiritual development, do you pray for radical change to take place in your life?
28. Do you then make the little daily changes needed that will ultimately lead to the larger changes you want?

BALANCE AND CONNECTION BETWEEN FISHES AREAS

Balance in your marriage, engagement, dating relationship, or individual life (if you are single) is critical, both at a personal level and at an overall relationship level. I encourage you to take the FISHES assessment once or twice a year. Be aware of where you currently rate on the one to ten scale for each category, as well as where you would like to be. Reflect on what you would define as a ten for you personally and what it would mean in terms of your marriage. If you are satisfied, and your spouse agrees, then give yourself a ten. You will find that the top priorities in life are interrelated and taking action in one area will impact the others. For example, if you would like to be a ten in the spiritual area, you must thoroughly understand and show to others the deeper meaning of love as described in Paul's first letter to the Corinthians 13:4–8, 13:

> Love is patient, love is kind. It is not jealous, (love) is not pompous, it is not inflated, it is not rude, it does not seek its own interests, it is not quick-tempered, it does not brood over injury, it does not rejoice over wrongdoing but rejoices with the truth. It bears all

things, believes all things, hopes all things, endures all things. Love never fails. If there are prophecies, they will be brought to nothing; if tongues, they will cease; if knowledge, it will be brought to nothing… So faith, hope, love remain, these three; but the greatest of these is love.

Living these words will also positively affect your family, social life, and health. FISHES can be a powerful growth exercise when you are open to your spouse's help. Because your spouse's viewpoint is based on what they actually observe of your actions and attitudes, their perspective can be particularly telling and insightful. As God's gift to you, your spouse will be your greatest transformational aid. Honest self-assessment and feedback from your spouse are critical to your growth, both as an individual and as a marriage partner. It is important to give them those opportunities to help you.

If you work to become a ten in each FISHES section, your marriage will be a source of immense joy, to you and to others. If not, your relationship could lead to a crisis. A few suggestions:

- Try to understand the reasons you rated as you did in each of your top priorities, as well as where you would like your scores to be.
- Identify any changes that may be necessary to affect your level of satisfaction.

- Demonstrate respect and consideration for your spouse by taking action and making the personal changes necessary to improve your marriage.
- Work together with your spouse to improve in specific areas—this will give you and your spouse an excellent opportunity to change and grow as one.

The first time I completed the FISHES assessment, my chart looked like something from a deformed fruit bin. My wife's chart looked equally distorted. However, as we worked together on our key issues and went through this exercise regularly, our levels of satisfaction increased and became more aligned. Most importantly, eventually, we learned that the key to improving our personal satisfaction and balance was to help each other.

A BLUEPRINT FOR MARRIAGE

SUCCESS MAPPING

When Elaine and I began to truly work together on developing a Christian marriage, we knew we needed more than just good intentions; we knew we needed a plan for success. It was clear that my old ways of ignoring her needs and the needs of the relationship were not going to work. Once I became willing to change and wanting to live a spiritual life, the Lord revealed to me that many of the secrets to building a good Christian marriage were not unlike finding success in most other areas of life. Through sharing and valuing each other's perspective, our task would be to understand our common goals. Only then, working together, could we develop the roadmap to a mutually happy marriage. This was an eye-opener and a tremendous relief.

Whether you want to build a sturdy structure, a resilient business, or a great marriage, there are few things more valuable than creating a blueprint or roadmap for success. This means going through a discovery process and not shying away from asking the tough questions:

- *Do you understand each other's expectations, and do you want the same things?* Start by taking the time to pray together that you will develop and agree on a plan that will serve as your source of power. Your blueprint can only be set when you both know what each other may want from the relationship. Clearly articulate your expectations, and commit to managing each other's expectations. Then work together to gain agreement on the key milestones, laying out the general timelines for reaching your agreed-upon expectations.

- *Have you determined your marriage priorities and agreed upon what are the most important?* Answer this by working together to build one set of priorities. You and your spouse will then have the power of a focused team operating in concert. Discuss your shared priorities and commit to gaining agreement on those that impact your marriage and family. The success of your marriage should take priority over personal priorities. To become one together in the Lord, you must remember that a great marriage is not about one person giving more or less than the other but each person giving 100 percent to their spouse and to the relationship.

- *What examples have you chosen to serve as your model?* Question what patterns may repeat themselves in your marriage. As discussed, many couples look to their parents' marriages as the model for married life. This may or may not be effective in today's world, or it may not even have been a good model to begin with. In the spirit of openness in becoming one in the Lord, read and discuss sections in Scripture that focus on marriage and relationship. Christ offered us His model for loving others through His teaching and the messages of His disciples. Reflect on your interpretations of John 15:12, the one commandment that Jesus gave us: "This is my commandment: love one another as I love you."

- *Have you vetted your plan with outside "experts"?* Always share your plan with a trusted mentor or spiritual advisor to know whether your blueprint is sound. In addition, talk with other Christian couples about marriage. Ask them questions regarding topics such as how they show love to one another, how they best communicate, and how they come to agreement over differences. Utilize and share in their wisdom and knowledge, learning from their mistakes, as well as the things that they have done to make their marriages thrive.

THE BASIC REQUIREMENTS OF WIVES AND HUSBANDS

An important part of the process in building the blueprint for a Christian marriage involves understanding a few of the key basic personal requirements that both men and women have for their spouse. A long time ago, someone sent me a list entitled "The Basic Needs of Women and Men." It was a very helpful tool, which I've used when working with married couples and couples in marriage preparation. It touches upon some of the key motivational differences between wives and husbands and what may drive their behaviors. Over the years I've made some changes to the list. Here is the adapted version.

A Wife's Basic Requirements

Women are blessed with a high degree of human sensitivity. A husband will become more appealing to his wife and strengthen his relationship with her by learning to understand and meet her needs:

1. *She wants to feel that she has a spiritual leader.* As his wife's chosen spiritual partner, the husband should take responsibility for leading his family to develop close, personal relationships with the Lord. He should embody the personal qualities of integrity, commitment, self-sacrifice, conviction, and consideration. Recognizing that her husband's character not only reflects on her but on the lives and futures of their children, the wife must believe that the choices and decisions that her husband will make are scripturally based and spiritually sound. As the primary teachers of their children, the husband and wife must partner in creating an environment for discussion and learning that encourages open discourse on spiritual matters. Because the wife wants her children to look to their father as a man of vision and spiritual conviction, as well as a man of his word, it is critical that the husband approach his responsibilities as spiritual leader of the home seriously and with reverence. Ephesians 5:23–27 makes

clear the husband's responsibility to personally embody the qualities of spiritual leader:

> For the husband is head of his wife just as Christ is head of the church, he himself the savior of the body. As the church is subordinate to Christ, so wives should be subordinate to their husbands in everything. Husbands, love your wives, even as Christ loved the church and handed himself over for her to sanctify her, cleansing her by the bath of water with the word, that he might present to himself the church in splendor, without spot or wrinkle or any such thing, that she might be holy and without blemish.

As a student of scripture, the husband must live according to the Bible's teachings so that he represents the Word of God. He should strive to be Christ-like. This high-caliber husband will serve his wife by leading her to become a woman of God, just as he will serve his family by leading their children in their spiritual training.

2. *She wants to feel affirmation for all she does and personally appreciated for the woman that she is.* As the most important man in a woman's life, it is the husband's duty to make sure that his wife feels recognized for all that she selflessly does for her husband and family. The husband must also continually praise his wife for her fine and virtuous personal qualities and character. Because she herself takes great pride in her abilities as a wife, mother, and homemaker, her

husband should openly and publicly praise his wife as a marvelous wife, mother, friend, lover, caretaker, and companion. The husband must make it clear to his wife that she is the most important woman in his life. In Proverbs 31:25–30, the importance of continually recognizing the character and works of the wife is clear:

She is clothed with strength and dignity, and she laughs at the days to come. She opens her mouth in wisdom, and on her tongue is kindly counsel. She watches the conduct of her household, and eats not her food in idleness. Her children rise up and praise her; her husband, too, extols her: "Many are the women of proven worth, but you have excelled them all." Charm is deceptive and beauty fleeting; the woman who fears the Lord is to be praised.

3. *She wants to feel romance and personal affection in her marriage.*

How beautiful you are, how pleasing,
my love, my delight!
Your very figure is like a palm tree,
your breasts are like clusters.
I said: I will climb the palm tree,
I will take hold of its branches.
Now let your breasts be like clusters of the vine
and the fragrance of your breath like apples,
And your mouth like an excellent wine
that flows smoothly for my lover,
spreading over the lips and the teeth.

In the Song of Solomon 7:7–10 an atmosphere of romance and the husband's appreciation for his wife is beautifully reflected. As his wife's courtier, hero, lover, and Prince Charming, the husband must cultivate an environment alive with the promise of generous affection and timely romantic expressions of love. The husband should continually show and tell his wife how deeply he cares for her. This can be done through actions such as giving flowers, cards, and gifts, playing a favorite song, praising her, and offering common, though thoughtful courtesies. It is important to remember that through affection and romance, a wonderful atmosphere for physical intimacy can be created.

4. *She wants to have intimate conversation with her husband.* As the man she trusts beyond all others, the husband must communicate with his wife at the feeling level in an open and heartfelt dialogue. He should ask her to reflect on the activities of her day, listening attentively with interest and sensitivity. These conversations will show that the husband values his wife's perspective. They also indicate his desire to simply understand her and not try to change her. The Song of Solomon 2:8–10, 14 poetically illustrates these intimate husband-wife conversations:

Hark! my lover-here he comes
springing across the mountains,
leaping across the hills.
My lover is like a gazelle

or a young stag.
Here he stands behind our wall,
gazing through the windows,
peering through the lattices.
My lover speaks; he says to me,
"Arise, my beloved, my beautiful one,
and come!...
O my dove in the clefts of the rock,
in the secret recesses of the cliff,
Let me see you,
let me hear your voice,
For your voice is sweet,
and you are lovely."

5. *She wants to feel there is openness and honesty in her marriage.* As his wife's confidant and best friend, the husband must encourage communications that are truthful and open through leading by example. In all areas of his life, he should confide in his wife with complete honesty. This will further strengthen her sense of security in him and her belief in what he says to her. Proverbs 15:22–23 spells out the value of this kind of transparency between trusted partners:

Plans fail when there is no counsel, but they succeed when counselors are many. There is joy for a man in his utterance; a word in season, how good it is!

Because the husband holds himself accountable to his wife, he explains his thoughts, intentions, plans, and actions openly and entirely. With love, he speaks to her directly, sharing his beliefs and ideas.

6. *She wants to feel she has stability and support at home.* A wife desires her husband to be a family man who takes all his responsibilities at home very seriously. This is stated in 1 Timothy 5:8:

And whoever does not provide for relatives and especially family members has denied the faith and is worse than an unbeliever.

He should strive to offer his family security and the promise for a better future, as well as emotional support and steadiness through tough times. If the wife has a job, career, or other obligations, the husband should commit to supporting his wife's interests and to helping her with household duties. The husband and wife working as a team are stronger and more intelligent as a whole than individually. When the husband backs up his wife's decisions dealing with family issues, she feels both respected for her views and actions and valued for what she brings to their home life.

7. *She wants to feel that her husband is committed to the family.* The peaceful order of how the family should be run is spelled out in Colossians 3:19–20:

Husbands, love your wives, and avoid any bitterness toward them. Children, obey your parents in everything, for this is pleasing to the Lord.

As a man prioritizing the needs of his family above his own personal needs or ambitions, the Christian husband demonstrates his commitment to "family first" by offering them his time and energy to help them with their spiritual, emotional, and intellectual development. Rather than focusing the majority of his available energy and time upon self-serving, greedy, or ambitious activities, and thus neglecting his wife and family in the process, the Christian family man becomes engaged in all levels of activities of his wife and children. These include sports, schoolwork, their clubs and groups, hobbies and interests, vacations and travel, their friends and social networks, and also prayer and church activities. Ephesians 6:4 asserts that the father must be committed to educating his children in the ways and teachings of the church:

> Fathers, do not provoke your children to anger, but bring them up with the discipline and instruction of the LORD.

A Husband's Basic Requirements

Men's needs are generally simple. A wife will engender herself deeply to her husband by learning to meet his basic requirements:

1. *He wants to feel his wife both admires and respects him.* As the spiritual partner she has chosen, as well as her man of the world, the husband should feel

that his wife values and appreciates his character, integrity, intellect, and personal capabilities and potential. Her support and guidance will help him feel that he has an equal partner in life who is on the same page with him in terms of what they can accomplish together. Having his wife be admiring and proud of him is one of the single greatest self-confidence boosters a man can have in his drive for married, personal, and professional success. Feeling his wife's uncompromising commitment to his success will inspire the husband to greatness and to love his wife unconditionally. Ephesians 5:33 makes this dynamic clear:

In any case, each one of you should love his wife as himself, and the wife should respect her husband.

2. *He wants to feel a physically intimate connection with his wife.* As her committed partner in marriage, the husband should feel that he and his wife bring physical intimacy into their relationship in ways that are satisfying and enjoyable to each. If she understands his specific requirements for intimacy, she will be better able to fulfill his desires. Once she understands her husband's needs, the wife should try to understand her own intimacy requirements and then share that information with her husband. Through open communication regarding each partner's needs, the couple can develop an intimate relationship that is both mutually fulfilling and emotionally inspiring. As described in 1 Corinthians

7:1–5, the importance of this requirement should never be overlooked or forgotten:

Now in regard to the matters about which you wrote: "It is a good thing for a man not to touch a woman," but because of cases of immorality every man should have his own wife, and every woman her own husband. The husband should fulfill his duty toward his wife, and likewise the wife toward her husband. A wife does not have authority over her own body, but rather her husband, and similarly a husband does not have authority over his own body, but rather his wife. Do not deprive each other, except perhaps by mutual consent for a time, to be free for prayer, but then return to one another, so that Satan may not tempt you through your lack of self-control.

As well as the inspirational benefits articulated in Proverbs 5:15–19:

Drink water from your own cistern, running water from your own well. How may your water sources be dispersed abroad, streams of water in the streets? Let your fountain be yours alone, not one shared with strangers; And have joy of the wife of your youth, your lovely hind, your graceful doe. Her love will invigorate you always, through her love you will flourish continually, When you lie down she will watch over you, and when you wake, she will share your concerns; wherever you turn, she will guide you.

3. *He wants to feel that he is supported at home and that his home life is stable.* A husband desires his wife to partner with him in creating a home environment that is peaceful, loving, restful, organized, and well run. Proverbs 21:19 makes this requirement abundantly clear:

It is better to dwell in a wilderness than with a quarrelsome and vexatious wife.

Their home should be their refuge. Even if she has a career or other outside responsibilities, a husband would like for his wife to partner in serving as the emotional and planning nexus for all activity related to the children's needs, the family's activities, and the order of the home.

4. *He wants to feel attracted to his wife.* The importance of a wife's attention to her appearance for her husband's benefit is expressed in 1 Peter 3:3–5:

Your adornment should not be an external one: braiding the hair, wearing gold jewelry, or dressing in fine clothes, but rather the hidden character of the heart, expressed in the imperishable beauty of a gentle and calm disposition, which is precious in the sight of God. For this is also how the holy women who hoped in God once used to adorn themselves and were subordinate to their husbands.

As his public and private "better half," the husband wants his wife to do all she can to take care of and present herself so that she is an attractive and well-spoken representation of him and their family. By always keeping herself in shape and tastefully attractive to her husband physically, mentally, and spiritually, the wife ensures that her husband will desire and appreciate her.

5. *He wants to feel that he has a life companion.* The desire for life companionship is evident in Song of Solomon 8:6:

Set me as a seal on your heart, as a seal on your arm;
For stern as death is love, relentless as the nether world is devotion; its flames are a blazing fire.

As his partner in marriage, the husband would like his wife to be his best friend. He would like for her to appreciate some of the activities he most enjoys, and for those interests that she does, they can take part in together. The wife should also encourage other activities, whether they are some of her favorite interests or if they are new, that they can mutually participate in and enjoy together. The key is for both to associate the activities they enjoy most with their spouse.

LIVING A CHRISTIAN MARRIAGE

As a deacon who works with couples, one of the most valuable instructions I try to give is that the basis to building a strong Christian marriage is through prioritizing God first and spouse second. This "God-first" foundation encompasses both developing a personal relationship with Jesus, as well as putting God at the center of their marriage.

Living Christ's teachings and being Christ-like will be the means for you and your spouse to develop this base. With the love and inspiration of Jesus' teachings guiding you, you will learn that there are many foundational steps you can take that will help you build your relationship into a Christian marriage. Some examples of these fundamental cornerstones are:

- Love that is unconditional
- Open and thoughtful communications
- Unqualified forgiveness
- Absolute friendship
- Commitment to fidelity
- Shared moments of prayer

The following is a list of several spiritually based actions you can take that will strengthen the foundation of your Christian marriage, as well as deepen your personal relationship with your spouse:

- *Say I Love You:* In my marriage seminars, I'll ask men how often they tell their wife that they love her. Many of them say, "I told her when we got married. Do I have to do it again?" The correct answer, for both husbands and wives, is "often." Taking the time to express your love to your spouse is an act of God.

- *Laugh Together:* Proverbs 17:22 tells us that: "A joyful heart is the health of the body, but a depressed spirit dries up the bones." Just about everyone has heard that laughter is the best medicine—and this certainly applies to relationships. It was a lesson I needed to learn firsthand. For many years I was quite grumpy about life, critical of those around me, and I rarely laughed. But once I turned my life over to Jesus, I asked God to help me become aware of the characteristics necessary for the happiness I lacked. He responded by telling me that I needed to develop a sense of humor about myself and the world. And so I began to seek out someone who I thought was funny in order to observe them in action. The man I began watching had the ability to make something funny out of almost anything. By observing him, God taught me how to laugh and to bring joy to others. I then shared my growing sense of humor with my wife, and we began learning to laugh together at the idiosyncrasies of life. We now laugh every day, and she has been my partner in comedy ever since.

- *Share Your Thoughts and Dreams:* Years ago I took an executive training course instructed by a man who had written a book on critical success factors in business. To the one hundred people in the class, the man instructed us on how to apply the key principles of strategic planning to our work. In the middle of his talk, he stopped and said, "I have to share something with you. I'm married and have a family. As I was writing this book on critical success factors, I started thinking about what has really been critical to my success. I began writing a list, and my wife wound up as the first success factor. I put my book down, drove home, and explained to my wife about the mental and writing exercise I had gone through that day. Then I told her that she was the most important thing in my life." This was a revelation to me. Until that day, I rarely shared any of my work or career-related ideas with my wife, much less any of my personal dreams. Now that Elaine and I strive to live as one in the LORD, I have found her to be my greatest counsel. I have learned that sharing my plans and dreams with her has opened a road to much greater vision.

- *Demonstrate Patience with Each Other:* In 1 Timothy 1:15–16, Paul explains the patience that God had shown to him in his transformation into an example of a born-again believer:

> This saying is trustworthy and deserves full acceptance: Christ Jesus came into the world to save sinners. Of these I am the foremost. But for that reason I was mercifully treated, so that in me, as the foremost, Christ Jesus might display all his patience as an example for those who would come to believe in him for everlasting life.

Although our human lifetimes on earth are limited, we are on a path to eternity. We must always remember that we are moving together with others along that path. If you think that you are ahead of your spouse on the path, take time to help your spouse get to the point where you are. If you are growing apart, then perhaps you are not spending enough time together helping each other. Jesus taught us to exercise patience and humility. In your spiritual journey, both you and your spouse should learn to work together as a team—each striving to help the other.

- *Pray:* Prayer is an unlimited source of power. Paul wrote in 1 Thessalonians 5:16–18 to:

    Rejoice always. Pray without ceasing. In all circumstances give thanks, for this is the will of God for you in Christ Jesus.

Paul encourages us to put on an attitude of prayer. He is encouraging us to strive to live our lives in continuous prayer, remembering that the Holy Spirit is always in us, ready to help us, without stopping or pausing, in all we do and think. Reflecting on life's challenges in silent prayer will give you perspective and understanding. As a daily activity of your marriage, engaging in prayer together will offer you both the opportunity to tap into that source of power. Reading the Bible together with an attitude of prayer will also help you look at life through the eyes of Christ. The Bible serves as a fountain of wisdom, and reflecting on Jesus' teachings will provide you both direction and courage.

- *Play:* Enjoying life and playing is the secret to staying young. As an annual exercise, my wife and I sit down together and make a list of all the things that we would like to do that year, including the trips we'd like to take and the places we want to visit. If we write down those plans early enough in the year, we actually go to some of the places and accomplish some of the things. Each year we've actually gotten better about not waiting to draft our list. Many successful couples use the aspects of play to plan their whole year and to define their time together. One couple that I worked with had desired to visit all 50 states. Thus far, they have traveled together to 49 of them.

- *Love:* Loving one another is Christ-like; it is the natural order of God's wish for humanity. Recall that Jesus' only commandment to us was that we love one another as He has loved us. Please remember that in everything you do, do in love. As your top earthly priority, your spouse should be the number one recipient of your love.

Remember that Christian marriages don't just happen—they are built through a combination of planning, maintaining a balanced approach, caring for each other's needs, and living a Christian life. Underscoring this will be your faith in Christ's teachings, which offer God's blueprint for a happy marriage. Building the ideal Christian marriage may take some sweat and elbow grease, but it will be well worth the effort and will stand the test of time.

DEALING WITH LIFE'S DIFFICULTIES

MAKING TIME FOR EACH OTHER

Like most couples, Elaine and I went through growing pains early in our relationship. During those first seven years, my focus was almost totally on myself, my career, and making money. I was totally consumed, and this left little time for my marriage. Elaine, likewise, had her hands full with raising a family, being involved with church, helping out with relatives, and generally putting up with me.

With the demands of modern life and the pace of change in our world, it can become easy to feel weighed down and overwhelmed. Making ends meet, caring for a family, advancing in a career, staying in shape, maintaining friendships, serving others, developing personal interests, staying current with e-mails and text messages, etc., all require time and focus. How should we face the challenges of living spirit-filled lives with all the demands the world places upon us? *The answer lies in where we place our priorities.* Matthew 6:24 tells us:

> No one can serve two masters. He will either hate one and love the other, or be devoted to one and despise the other. You cannot serve God and mammon.

Why are you so busy? Do financial goals dictate your perceptions of happiness? Do you feel as though you are not in control of your life? Are the things that matter most (spiritual life, family, and friends) getting the leftovers of your time?

Check these symptoms:

1. You have a list of topics to discuss but no time to discuss them.
2. You're going to bed later and are more tired when you get up.
3. You keep thinking things will slow down next week, the following week, or then maybe the week after that.
4. You make excuses for why you're so busy.
5. You're more irritable and grouchy.
6. You feel overburdened with the responsibilities of work and/or other activities (church, school, sports, civic, social, etc.)
7. You and your spouse have little energy left for each other.

If this list sounds familiar, then it is probably time to make some changes. As your guide, go back to your list of priorities. God will not give you more than you can handle, and He certainly does not intend for you to be too busy for your spouse and family. Sit down together with your spouse and reevaluate your activities. When setting your daily and weekly schedules, be sure to block out time for just the two of you. Remember that other than Christ, your spouse is your top priority and attention to your relationship is your number one responsibility. Saint Paul tells us in Ephesians 5:25–30:

> Husbands, love your wives, even as Christ loved the church and handed himself over for her to sanctify her, cleansing her by the bath of water with the word, that he might present to himself the church in splendor, without spot or wrinkle or any such thing, that she might be holy and without blemish. So (also) husbands should love their wives as their own bodies. He who loves his wife loves himself. For no one hates his own flesh but rather nourishes and cherishes it, even as Christ does the church, because we are members of his body.

One of the best solutions to the "I'm too busy" syndrome is to *make time daily for prayer,* both alone and together with your spouse. Prayer serves as a reminder to put God first in your life. Prayer also offers the gift of perspective. When meditating on Scripture or communicating with God, time sometimes seems to stand still. Sowing more time into prayer and scripture will actually multiply your time and will provide focus on those things that are most important to you. Find a time every day for you and your spouse to pray together.

When Elaine and I pray together, it gives us both a sense of unity as we ask God to bless our family. We have found that a powerful way to start our day is to pray our morning prayers together. This helps us both to be on the same page around the demands of the day. If you have a particularly busy or challenging day ahead, pray first—you will reap many benefits. It will allow you to share your thoughts, hopes, concerns, and plans with your loving Spiritual Father and to understand His agenda for your day. Proverbs 2:3–6 makes the promise clear that through earnest prayer will come an understanding of God's Will:

> Yes, if you call to intelligence, and to understanding raise your voice; If you seek her like silver, and like hidden treasures search her out: Then will you understand the fear of the Lord; the knowledge of God you will find; For the Lord gives wisdom, from his mouth come knowledge and understanding…

When planning your time and activities, keep in mind your top priorities in life and arrange your schedule accordingly. Ask yourself:

1. How do you measure where you are placing focus?
2. Are the decisions you are making around time management filtered through your priorities and aspirations?
3. To whom or what are you giving your primary attention?

As one of your top priorities, dedicated relationship time with your spouse should be planned. Know that time alone with your spouse is critical to growing the relationship. When Elaine and I plan our weekly calendars and daily schedules, we are now very careful to allot time for each other. Since we are both quite busy, having filters on how we decide to spend our time has helped us to both grow our relationship and be more productive. We've found that by setting time limits on activities, we are able to get much more done. My own personal priorities and filters are God, family and friends, church activities, work, and golf—in that order. *How I balance these is critical.* I have to be mindful of managing my time so that no single activity overshadows the others.

One example of a priority that can become all-encompassing is church. As a deacon, I've had to learn to set specific time limits around my ministry activities. While ministering and providing spiritual assistance to others is important, I know that God does not intend for it to be above the needs of my own family. Ephesians 5:33 tells us, "In any case, each one of you should love his wife as himself, and the wife should respect her husband."

Here are some helpful rules of thumb for getting more out of your time together:

- *Offer quality time:* Don't make each other settle for time leftovers at the end of the day.
- *Date night:* Plan a weekly (or at least a monthly) date night for you and your spouse to spend time together away from the rest of the family. It is important to

spend some dedicated time together outside of daily routines and activities. This needs not to be expensive. A cup of coffee, a hamburger, or even a walk in the park all make great inexpensive dates.

- *Share meals together:* Set a goal for sharing a meal with your family at least five times a week. Remember the importance that Jesus put on breaking bread with those you love.

- *Use time twice:* By doing household and family tasks together (the dishes, yard work, etc.) or by driving to meetings or activities together, you'd be surprised how much time with your spouse you'd have to share your thoughts and feelings and to discuss your day.

- *Show love through affection:* The human touch between two people who love each other has a wonderfully healing and spiritual effect. My personal goal is to give my spouse at least eight hugs and five kisses a day

- *Lighten up and have fun:* Don't take life or yourself too seriously. It's amazing how being a little more laid back and using smiles and laughter instead of frowns and criticism will not only bring you closer but also will engender a new life spirit and freshness to your relationship.

It's no secret that those couples that make time for each other have the most successful marriages. God wants us to be both successful in our careers and to have happy marriages. However, it doesn't just happen. It is up to you to make it a top priority.

MANAGING CONFLICTS

Disagreements, misunderstandings, and differences of opinion will always be a part of living in a society. They are unavoidable. Conflict exists everywhere in this world—between nations, between rivals, between allies and enemies—essentially anywhere two or more parties may have competing interests. This includes marriage. However, married couples that learn to deal with conflict and disagreement through the teachings of Christ have an opportunity to transform and fortify their relationship.

Conflicts in marriages can arise from many sources, with some of the most common being:

- Finances
- Approach to raising children
- Control issues
- Poor communication
- Household responsibilities
- Sexual issues
- Infidelity
- Emotional neglect
- Inconsideration
- Self-centeredness
- Spirituality

These are in our world and in marriages for a special reason: *Though difficult, conflicts represent tremendous opportunities for growth*. The manner in which we deal with conflict offers us the prospect of rising above our personal and human shortcomings and fulfilling the greater personal potential that Christ has written for us. Nothing is written in stone saying that conflict has to be something negative. A positive and constructive approach to conflict can bring spouses closer together and can strengthen the foundation of the marriage.

A proactive way of addressing conflict, of course, is to not create it in the first place. By learning to act from a place of love, accepting others, and respecting the laws of society, you can avoid much unnecessary discord in life. In Matthew 22:16–17, the Pharisees and the Herodians attempted to trick Christ into speaking against the law of Caesar and thus inciting rebellion when they asked:

> Teacher, we know that you are a truthful man and that you teach the way of God in accordance with the truth. And you are not concerned with anyone's opinion, for you do not regard a person's status. Tell us, then, what is your opinion: Is it lawful to pay the census tax to Caesar or not?

In earthly matters of minimal spiritual significance, Christ instructed his followers *to follow the rules and the law of the land*. As explained in the next verses, Matthew 22:18–22:

> Knowing their malice, Jesus said, "Why are you testing me, you hypocrites? Show me the coin that pays the census tax." Then they handed him the Roman coin. He said to them, "Whose image is this and whose

inscription?" They replied, "Caesar's." At that he said to them, "Then repay to Caesar what belongs to Caesar and to God what belongs to God." When they heard this they were amazed, and leaving him they went away.

Paul's teachings also chart out a plan for harmonious living. In Romans 13:8–9, he instructs:

> Owe nothing to anyone, except to love one another; for the one who loves another has fulfilled the law. The commandments, "You shall not commit adultery; you shall not kill; you shall not steal; you shall not covet," and whatever other commandment there may be, are summed up in this saying, (namely) "You shall love your neighbor as yourself."

When Christ is at the center of your marriage, there is no room for conflict—issues for discussion do not become points of contention. Problem areas can be addressed before becoming major crises or sources of contention. In a Christ-centered marriage, when you and your spouse commit to living the words of Scripture, conflict actually becomes an exercise of growth and self-discovery. *You will be able to recognize disagreements as an opportunity to better understand each other's needs.* Also know that your relationship is worth more than whatever you may be discussing.

Diagram: Living a Christ-Centered Marriage

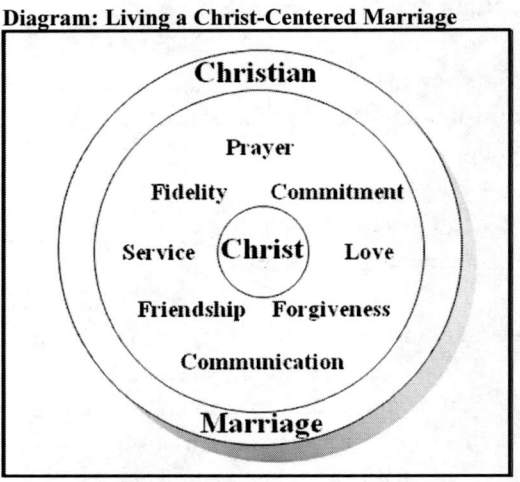

When disagreements or differences of opinion do arise, crises can often be avoided if issues are discussed and decisions made early on. Don't avoid or ignore any issues that may pose potential problems or conflicts. Procrastination rarely works. As to where to begin, look to the FISHES areas of priority and expectations in Chapter Five: Living a Balanced Life. Because these are the most basic needs, strong differences of opinion that are left unaddressed can eventually become conflicts. *The sooner you begin working toward agreement on your priorities, the sooner you can begin crafting compromises.* In Ephesians 4:26–27, Paul advises:

> Be angry but do not sin; do not let the sun set on your anger, and do not leave room for the devil.

Several years ago Elaine complained to me about my habit of squeezing the toothpaste in the middle of the tube. By her speaking up as to what was bothering her, I was able take corrective action; I went out and bought Elaine her own tube. Now she no longer complains about the toothpaste. Plus, we don't even have to use the same brand!

This little example shows how the ease and value of addressing issues when they first appear and not letting tensions build up. As an analogy, when your car's "add oil" light comes on, it's a good idea to add oil or have it serviced as quickly as possible. One could say that marriages are a lot like cars in that sense. However, good marriages usually get better mileage.

One of the great blessings that God has given Elaine and me over the course of our marriage has been our learning to work through problem issues and to resolve our conflicts and challenges. Having read this far, you have a pretty good idea that it didn't quite start out that way.

What an adventure! Through the journey of our marriage, we've worked our way into and through many, many conflicting situations and issues. Christ's teachings have been the torch that has led us through the storms. In the end, these challenges have given us greater understanding and insight into each other and into our selves.

CONSTRUCTIVELY COMMUNICATING

> *Once upon a time,* there was a young couple named Tom and Elaine who had a somewhat-rocky marriage, due in part to a communication issue. Although Tom thought of himself at the time to be a dazzling communicator,

Elaine's perception of Tom's communication style was a bit different. She would have probably even described it as argumentative. Elaine's communication style, though equally potent, was much more listener-friendly and laidback. The difference in their communication approaches eventually became a source of conflict in their relationship.

Just like most couples that learn to become happily married, Elaine and Tom needed to discover how to discuss difficult issues and disagreements constructively in order to have a growing and peaceful marriage. They wanted to find a common ground for communicating that would allow for each to share their opinions and ideas without confrontation. *Both wanted to feel that their viewpoint was respected and acknowledged, though neither felt as if they were getting through…*

Yes, that was our story. When faced with the possibility of losing our marriage, I forced myself to become open to change. Communication had been a weakness in our relationship. I prayed for an understanding of how to create an environment where Elaine and I would feel comfortable sharing openly. I prayed for insight on how to better manage discussions of problem issues.

As I then drew closer to Christ, the secret knowledge was revealed: *Focus our relationship around Jesus' teachings and the problems and differences in our communication styles of the past would become less relevant.* Once I began communicating with Elaine more constructively, creating an atmosphere of love and listening, as well as speaking, she, in turn, became interested in hearing my perspectives.

As we both have grown in our faith and understanding of Christ's teachings, we've discovered how much more we are in-tune with each other's needs. While it's important to communicate honestly on problem issues, I have learned to do so in ways that are less than brutally honest. Part of my personal journey and growth has been to develop more effective communication techniques. Scripture has been my guide. As Paul teaches us in 1 Corinthians 12:3, that which is in our hearts will guide what is spoken through our lips:

> Therefore, I tell you that nobody speaking by the spirit of God says, "Jesus be accursed." And no one can say, "Jesus is LORD," except by the Holy Spirit.

The following are three communication techniques that Elaine and I have put into practice in our marriage. They provide a framework for discussing issues and offer an agreed-upon system for feedback:

- *Set a Routine:* In order to stay on top of the latest issues in our relationship, Elaine and I try to follow a "communications agenda." In addition to discussing current matters around family, church, careers, finances, etc., we also discuss concerns that may have been originally overlooked, such as behaviors and habits. *This gives us the opportunity to address ongoing issues before they become conflicts.* Privacy and discretion are also critical to communication in marriage. When an issue comes up that may pose a conflict, the first thing we do is establish how and when we will address it. We've found that it is never a good idea to correct your spouse in public or in front of the children, other family members, or friends.

- *Communicate the Issues:* When addressing difficult subjects, keep the discussion focused on the problem or issue. This is more constructive than focusing on the individual, which can feel like a personal attack. Elaine and I learned long ago that separating the issue from the individual is vital to keeping our communications productive and positive. Additionally, when discussing a problem issue, we try to look at the conflict from the big-picture perspective. Is the conflict a symptom of another issue? Is the real issue about finances, priorities, expectations, etc.? If it is, our conversation would be more productive once focused on the larger concern and not on the symptom.

- *Give Feedback Scores:* Continual assessment and feedback is the way in which we let each other know how we are doing in the communications department. Because we trust each other's perspective and are committed to helping each other grow, our approach has been somewhat unique. In our kitchen we have a chalkboard with both of our names written on it for keeping score. Any time I say or do something that deserves feedback, Elaine can go to the chalkboard and rate how I'm doing on a scale from 1 to 10, and vice versa. Just like having assignments graded and receiving report cards in school, actually seeing feedback on current performance can be quite effective.

So while "once upon a time" our communication was a source of conflict, it is now a source of comfort and the lifeblood of our relationship.

TAKING RESPONSIBILITY FOR NEGATIVE EMOTIONS

Another area critical to managing conflict is learning to deal with anger and negative emotions. Conflict thrives on negative emotions, and married couples and individuals that let their emotions run rampant also run the risk of bringing unnecessary conflict and stress into their relationships. Take personal responsibility for learning how to deal with emotions such as anger.

Many years ago, traffic and bad drivers were my stimulus hot buttons. I would get angry after being cut-off or slighted by an inconsiderate driver. My reaction was an outpouring of emotion and anger, which upset Elaine greatly. The turning point was when she and I discussed this, and she shared how my emotional reactions made her feel. Once I recognized the effect it had on her, I committed to resolving this source of conflict in our marriage. I immediately adopted a more Christian approach to my driving—being calmer, more laidback, less reactive, and much more giving and polite. That stimulus is no longer a source of conflict in either of our lives. I learned that taking personal responsibility for my life and actions, anger and other negative emotions become more manageable.

There are a few key techniques that we practice to help us keep emotions in check and allow us to work through our issues constructively:

- *Do not get angry at the same time:* It's always a good idea to try having one person keep a cool head.
- *Do not interrupt or talk over the other person while they are angry or upset:* Raise your hand or have a nonverbal signal when wanting a turn to speak.
- *Do not go to bed angry:* Work toward a resolution, but at the end of the night, let go of whatever anger may still be there.

Avoiding anger and negative emotions is not the solution—a marriage is not good just because one or both spouses never get angry. Some couples just endure and go on about carrying the crosses of their misery. In working with married couples, I've actually encountered many who believed "God didn't intend for us to have a happy marriage." How ridiculous! The truth is that God wants everyone to have wonderful, happy, and fulfilling marriages. *He sent his Son into our world to show us the way.*

PRACTICING FORGIVENESS

Jesus taught the most important and effective means for managing conflict: forgiveness. Being imperfect humans, we will always be vulnerable to sources of conflict: things will be misunderstood, disagreements will crop up, tensions will rise, and mistakes will be made. But by living and sharing the love taught by Christ, we elevate ourselves above conflicts and problems. If you practice the forgiveness that Jesus preached in Luke 6:35–36, you will be on a path to inner peace and happiness:

> But rather, love your enemies and do good to them, and lend expecting nothing back; then your reward will be great and you will be children of the Most High, for he himself is kind to the ungrateful and the wicked. Be merciful, just as (also) your Father is merciful.

As you work together through difficult issues, demonstrate your love for your spouse by exercising patience, tolerance, and forgiveness. If these are a challenge, pray for God's help in allowing the necessary changes to happen within you. In 1 Corinthians 13:4–7, Paul wrote of love and forgiveness:

> Love is patient, love is kind. It is not jealous, (love) is not pompous, it is not inflated, it is not rude, it does not seek its own interests, it is not quick-tempered, it does not brood over injury, it does not rejoice over wrongdoing but rejoices with the truth. It bears all things, believes all things, hopes all things, endures all things.

Practicing forgiveness in your marriage is a good barometer of how well you deal with difficult issues and potential conflicts in general.

Remember that life is a journey and that God intends for it to be an adventure. Working through challenges and managing conflicts in your relationship is the tempering that will help it to stand the test of time. How we handle conflict is a meaningful way in which God allows us to exercise free will. He has given us many options; we can choose to seek out a compromise, impose our will, give in to the will of others, run from conflict, seek revenge, etc. However, it is by striving for compromises and win-win solutions that both parties can reach positive outcomes. They are usually much more productive than "I win" or "you win" outcomes. God wants you both to win.

Putting Christ first in your life and at the center of your marriage will make this a natural action. It will help you and your spouse to develop communication styles that are complementary and not conflicting. It will help you in dealing with anger and negative emotions. It will show you the power of forgiveness. Differences of opinion, disagreements, and even conflict in your marriage do not have to be unproductive. They represent an unavoidable chance for developing and opportunities for transformational growth. Why, if not for Goliath, David would have remained just a shepherd!

WORKING TOGETHER

For the first several years of our marriage, Elaine and I were on separate paths. As I've described, her focus was on raising our family and being a good wife, and mine was on money and career. A pitfall that some husbands and wives fall into is the expectation that their spouse is there to serve them and make them happy. And yes, I certainly was a case in point. Before I had my personal revelation and decided that I needed to change, I believed that it was Elaine's responsibility to make my life easier. My justification was that because I was serving as the breadwinner for the family, the household duties were not my domain. After a long day of work, I expected dinner to be on the table, the kids cleaned up and put to bed, and all matters related to the household to be in order. Looking back, how she found the patience to endure those early years of our marriage was itself a miracle. Thankfully, God's love intervened. He taught me several valuable lessons regarding the need for my wife and me to work together.

A key ingredient to having a successful marriage is unconditional love. As Jesus teaches in the Gospel of John, we should love others as we would love ourselves. This offers a key insight into working together to create a happy marriage—to love and serve one's spouse as we would want to be loved and served, expecting nothing in return. A spouse should never be treated like a servant or be expected to bring happiness. Marriage is a partnership, with the most important condition being to love without condition. It is the first of the fruits of the Spirit.

A second key ingredient is for spouses to work together as equals when facing the challenges of life. As explored throughout this book, good marriages are by no means an accident; they are the result of two partners, each with different strengths and skills, acting as one in the pursuit of common priorities and goals. This requires a 100 percent commitment to the relationship, putting Christ at the center of the marriage and living the lessons and teachings of Scripture.

A third key to working together is to set fair and realistic expectations when it comes to the sharing of household tasks and familial activities. I recently read a study that said 25 percent of married couples share their home life duties sixty-forty and that those couples report greater overall satisfaction and happiness than couples with a less balanced sharing of household duties. Couples should sit down and discuss what needs to be done and agree upon priorities. Responsibilities should be divided so that neither spouse feels overwhelmed. Additionally, each spouse should feel as though their areas of responsibility are just as important as those of their spouse. Respect and appreciation for each other's duties is central. It promotes teamwork and motivates each spouse to carry out their responsibilities with love and pride. Completing the bare minimum to get by should not be the goal. When sharing the workload and helping one another, couples should go the extra mile and give a little bit more. As Jesus directed in the Sermon on the Mount (Matthew 5:41), "Should anyone press you into service for one mile, go with him for two miles."

An additional way that Elaine and I have learned to avoid conflict over household chores involves having a plan and timeline for our "honey do" list. Knowing that there would always be repairs, maintenance, and chores that she'd like completed around the house, and knowing that in order to save money I would prefer to do the work myself, we decided to regularly sit down together and make out a list and date it. Then after thirty days, if I have not completed an item on the list, she has my full support to go ahead and hire painters, plumbers, work crews, etc., to get the job done. Now every time I complete an item from the list, I hug and kiss my wife, and we're both happy. Likewise, if after thirty days my only progress has been a trip to the store to buy paint or materials, we will still be standing there holding hands and happy as we comment on what a nice job the work crews are doing finishing up the job. Thus, there is no argument either way, as we have a plan for how to get things done.

And finally, when one's spouse—or virtually anyone, for that matter—does something kind or thoughtful, it is invaluable to share the love of Christ by showing gratitude. It is a sign of appreciation and respect. Gratitude shows that the effort has been recognized. First Timothy 4:4 teaches us, "For everything created by God is good, and nothing is to be rejected when received with thanksgiving."

When Elaine and I began to deal with our marital and family issues as a unified team, we learned the strength of partnership. We found each of the four key ingredients discussed in this section (unconditional love, working as equals, setting realistic expectations, and showing gratitude) to be integral to the transformation of our marriage. With our love for Christ as the foundation for our marriage, we've learned how to find the peace and joy in working through life's challenges together, a fifth key ingredient. We've found that this has also given us twice the perspective into any problem or situation. When it comes to major issues and family questions, we share our thoughts and feelings, decide together what must be done, and then present a solid, unified front going forward. This has helped us to build trust and faith in our partnership, as well as to leverage each other's strengths working together as a team.

A GREAT MARRIAGE IS LIFE CHANGING

BRINGING HOME THE JOY

The day Elaine and I married was the most joyful day in our lives. With all the hope and promise of building a life together and starting a family, we walked down that aisle as if we were embarking upon an incredible adventure, and, in all reality, we were. We were the most important people in each other's life, and we knew that we had found the perfect partner for our future. It was to be a future of love, peace, wisdom, joy, fun, and all the fruit of the Holy Spirit.

The thrill of new beginnings, however, began to fade over time. As we became more accustomed to each other and to being "a married couple," the weeks and months and years of new, competing priorities dimmed the excitement of an unlimited future. As I've described throughout my testimony, I became fixated on my needs and furthering my career. Unfortunately for my wife and children, who viewed me as their spiritual leader, neither of these brought any real joy to our household. I became serious, driven, critical, and demanding, not to mention angry about something most of the time. There was little joy.

Faced with the daily misery of an unloving, unappreciative husband, Elaine finally decided that enough was enough. Her life had become unbearable. She drew her line in the sand and said, "Tommy, I want a divorce."

That was my turning point. That was the splash of ice water in the face I needed. The threat of losing my family, the people I really did love at the time, awoke me to the reality that I was going to have to change. Although I knew that there was no quick fix, I became inspired to transform our household from joyless shell to a home of love, warmth, fun, kindness, sharing, and compassion. The change had to start with me. The lesson I learned, the inspiration that transformed me was this: I must let go of my self-centered focus and live to bring joy and happiness to my family and those I love.

In John 15: 13, Jesus said, "Greater love has no one than this, that one lay down his life for his friends."

In the typical marriage ceremony, a key moment in the marriage vows comes when the bride and groom commit to being there for the other in good times and bad, in sickness and in health, until death do they part. When each says this, what they are actually committing to is a promise to lay down their own life for the life of their spouse. Self-sacrifice in marriage can take many forms, but at its essence, it is placing higher value on our spouse's needs and happiness than our own personal wants and desires. While this concept may not be something heralded in modern society and popular culture, it is critical to finding and sharing meaningful, lasting joy. Mother Teresa of Calcutta said it beautifully:

> Spread love everywhere you go, first of all in your own house. Give love to your children, to your wife or husband, to a next door neighbor. Let no one ever come to you without leaving better and happier. Be the living expression of God's kindness; kindness in your face, kindness in your eyes, kindness in your smile, kindness in your warm greeting.

Unfortunately for some marriages, the beauty of Jesus' "no greater love" promise is missed or forgotten. The opposite of you laying down your life for someone else would be you expecting to be served, as well as expecting others to make you happy. When practiced in marriage, one or both spouses may expect that their own personal happiness is dependent upon the actions of the other. Then, when the expectation is missed, both spouses may become critical and bitter. Having given the responsibility for their own happiness to something beyond their personal control, they may begin blaming others and assuming a victim mentality. Rather than affecting the external, they have allowed the external to affect them. This is a sacrifice of personal freedom and responsibility.

Our human nature is to be caught up in our own selfishness and wanting our own way. For unhappily married couples, there is usually little focus or effort to bring happiness to the relationship. Nor do these couples believe that their spouses are indeed wonderful gifts sent by a loving God. "Where is *my* joy? When am I going to be happy?" they may ask. The irony of this is that nothing offers fulfillment like bringing joy to others. Thus, rather than looking to the external for fulfillment, look inside for what you can share to enhance the lives of others. This is critical to *taking responsibility for your own happiness.* In Luke 11:10, Jesus teaches us, "For everyone who asks receives; he who seeks finds; and to him who knocks, the door will be opened."

How much more the Father will give to those who make the effort! The message here is for you to take action by bringing joy to others rather than expecting it to come from them. One of the questions in the FISHES assessment is, "What would it be like to be married to me?" Look at your relationship from your spouse's perspective. Would there be joy, contentment, respect, thankfulness? Are you now willing to commit to giving yourself fully to the marriage?

Although focusing on creating happiness for your spouse may at first seem unnatural, this fundamental change will transform your life and marriage in ways you've never dreamed. As you do this, you will enjoy increased self-respect and personal pride in making your spouse happy. Once you begin offering joy, love, and happiness without any expectation of it being returned, you have significantly changed your life. You will have transformed from being selfish to being selfless. This is at the core of all unconditional love. Your own happiness will grow from openly spreading joy and helping others. You will be bringing joy everywhere you go!

Joy is not the absence of sorrow—joy is the presence of God. You are not holy because you have the Holy Spirit; you are holy because the Holy Spirit has you. This means that you have given yourself over to the will of God, letting His love work through you in serving others. Couples that work together to follow God's plan for marriage let the Spirit within them bring joy to each other. This shared happiness through sacrifice is at the core of Christ's "no greater love" teaching. *It is at the core of two becoming one.*

People often ask Elaine and me about what things we recommend they do to bring happiness to their spouses and better serve their marriages. Here are some valuable steps we offer as suggestions if you would like to bring more joy into your marriage:

- *Become best friends:* The secret to making your spouse your best friend is to do all you can to become *their* best friend. There is truth to the old adage that to find a friend, be a friend. Think about what your spouse would be looking for in a best friend, and then *be* that friend to them. Forty years ago, when Elaine and I were both focused on our individual needs and not each other's, being each other's best friend wasn't even on the radar. We both already had several best friends, which unfortunately at the time did not include the person to whom we were married. However, we recognized that our relationship would need to change if we were to find greater happiness. We both wanted a joyous, loving, fulfilling marriage, so we began listening to each other's needs and expectations around communicating, trusting, sharing, and not feeling judged. After we began to understand what each other sought in a best friend, it shouldn't be a surprise that we eventually became each other's greatest pal. While having circles of close friends we trust and know intimately has clearly been a blessing, becoming each other's best friend has given us even greater fulfillment. This best friend is a gift from God.

- *Grow spiritually together:* Married couples that are able to help each other grow in their faith are better able to transcend selfishness and have stronger marriages than those who do not. Here are some interesting statistics:

    1. The overall divorce rate in the US is 50 percent. The average marriage lasts less than ten years.

    2. However, the divorce rate for couples who go to church together is one in fifty.

    3. The divorce rate for couples who pray together daily is one in one thousand.

Being an active participant in your spouse's spiritual development will bring you closer together and more in-tune with the wonderful plan God has for the both of you. One of the smartest decisions I've made was to give my wife the right to help me to be more like Christ. And she has done the same. By giving each other constructive, loving feedback on how Christ-like we are living our lives, Elaine and I stay actively involved in each other's spiritual growth. Through the years, this has paid off handsomely, both in the joy that it has brought to our relationship and to our ability to bring joy to others. God's plan for us is to grow to become more like Jesus, not like each other. We are born with selfish, inward-looking natures. However, God loves us and wants us to transcend our immaturity and learn the nature of the Holy Spirit. That is why we must be reborn, as Jesus teaches Nicodemus in John 3:3: "Amen, amen, I say to you, no one can see the kingdom of God without being born from above."

By bringing Christ into the center of our marriage, we have been able to help each other be born again in Christ and have a better understanding of the potential lives God has given us. Some of the ways in which we do this are by praying together daily, attending mass together each week, giving each other Christ-based instruction and feedback, working together with other couples who are trying to live Christian lives, sharing our Scripture study lessons together, and by continually discussing our plans for strengthening our faith. The key has been to help each other grow in Christ.

- *Respect and deal with feelings and emotions:* Couples that are actively tuned into each other's feelings are better able to work through the difficulties in life and marriage. Active verbal communication is the medium through which couples must share what they are thinking and feeling. Typically, women do this much better than men. I once read a study which reported that women speak 25,000 words a day and that men speak only 12,500 words a day. That's a two-to-one differential in communication styles! It kind of makes you wonder how men and women can communicate as well as they do with that kind of verbal gap. While emotions can have a liberating influence on communication between spouses, they can also be an inhibitor. Learn to deal with negative emotions, such as anger, and how to handle conflict, as discussed in Chapter

Seven: Dealing with Life's Difficulties. Look and live facing forward, and do not dwell upon the past. Communication can often become blocked by pains from the past that have not been forgiven. This is where Christ's message of forgiveness in Matthew 6:14–15 can help open things up and begin the healing:

> If you forgive others their transgressions, your heavenly Father will forgive you. But if you do not forgive others, neither will your Father forgive your transgressions.

Let go of the pain from the past by absolving those involved and decide to move forward with your life. Christ loves our emotional sides and wants us to be in touch with and deal with our feelings. Embrace the idea that feelings and emotions are an important part of communication between happily married couples. Listen, share, and be in tune with each other's feelings. The respect that each spouse has for the other's feelings and emotions is one of the most significant factors determining whether a marriage survives and grows. Here are some guiding points for putting emotions and feelings to good use while communicating:

- Give your spouse your full attention
- Be flexible and tolerant
- Discuss ideas and issues without criticism
- Talk with your spouse, not at your spouse
- Agree that only one of you can be upset at a time
- Have a good and positive attitude

- Be completely honest when you share
- Agree to disagree
- Keep a sense of humor and don't be afraid to laugh at yourself
- Strive for mutual satisfaction in the conversation

Negotiating through difficult times and issues requires both spouses to respect and care about the emotions of the other. Trust that Christ is with you as you and your spouse learn to embrace your emotional sides and respect the role that feelings can play in effective communication.

- *Develop and share common interests:* Ever notice that some of your best friends are people with whom you like doing things that interest you? Whether it is work, hobbies, politics, church, sports, travel, etc., having someone to share these experiences with makes them all the more meaningful and enjoyable. As your God-given gift, your spouse is your greatest pal and companion for experiencing the journey of life.

A critical element to making your marriage successful and fulfilling will be to cultivate interests in activities and pursuits in which you can share. How you and your spouse approach this is important. For most couples, activities can be grouped into two categories: (1) the things in which you both have an interest, and (2) the things in which one spouse has an interest but must pursue individually because their partner has no interest. The point I'd like to make in this section is that there is a third category, one that resonates with the "Bringing Home the Joy" theme of this chapter. Instead of each spouse only pursuing what they like, those couples who are committed to having stronger marriages should work on *cultivating interests in some of each other's favorite activities and pursuits.* This embodies what Jesus taught in Matthew 5:41: "Should anyone press you into service for one mile, go with him for two miles."

Go the extra mile for your spouse, and take an interest in those things in which they feel passionate. The benefits are tremendous:

- Your spouse will feel respected as an individual.
- You are showing your commitment to putting your spouse's needs ahead of your own.
- Your spouse will feel honored that you are genuinely interested in the pursuits that they hold dear.
- And finally, you both will have a heck of a lot of fun doing a new set of activities together, learning new things, gaining new perspectives and knowledge, and bringing home joy to each other.

Because most couples are usually very busy with their careers, children, chores, and duties, take the valuable time you have together with your spouse and make it worthwhile. Spend time together exploring life, do things together that encourage personal growth, and share in each other's spiritual development.

One of the pitfalls that many marriages fall victim to is stagnation, where the relationship ceases to grow and the daily routine becomes robotic and complacent. After forty-seven years of marriage, Elaine and I still genuinely "date" each other. This has been a key insight into our long-term happiness. It's as if we try to be in continual "courting mode" and work to win the attention, affection, trust, laughter, and love of the other. Couples that continue to date after they are married, focusing on each other's needs and spending quality time together, are better able to share the joys of life together. Courtship after marriage and cultivating interest in each other's favorite activities indeed takes time, but the return is enormous. Importantly, it takes less time to maintain a loving relationship than it does to repair a broken one. Thus, take the time to laugh, play, dream, and share—all secrets to staying young.

When both you and your spouse work together to bring joy to one another, you are powerfully transforming your marriage and yourselves. God gave us our precious gifts of life and talents to spread happiness, kindness, and love, not to be selfish and self-focused. If you are a Christian couple baptized in the Holy Spirit, others should be able to observe your happiness and witness the love you and your spouse share. Luke 11:13 says, "If you then, who are wicked, know how to give good gifts to your children, how much more will the Father in heaven give the holy Spirit 5 to those who ask him?"

You have made the decision to love and to serve one another, thus implementing an important part of God's plan for a successful and Christ-centered marriage. As taught by Mother Teresa, you and your marriage have become transformed into the living expression of God's love and kindness.

RELATIONSHIPS 101: MARRIAGE AS A MODEL FOR ALL RELATIONSHIPS

Through Jesus Christ, the Lord gave us a perfect model for living, for loving others, and for laying down our lives in service to a greater good. This path was not easy. Jesus continually prayed that He could be like the Father, yearning for a greater understanding of God's will and asking humbly for help through His ministry and transformation. Through His teachings and sacrifice, Jesus became the embodiment of love, the extreme example God gave us to show how we should relate to others. Through his death and resurrection, Jesus became the supreme model for change and rebirth.

In the Catholic Church, we think of purgatory as a place of positive transformation. Because we believe that a person will be transformed into a loving being—living and sharing the fruit of the Spirit—before they experience the presence of God in heaven, purgatory serves as that state of alteration.

This reminds me of a story I often tell about making the most of your time for transformation. One day while praying, I thanked God for all the blessings I had been given, particularly for my having had a long and successful career in computers. God responded by saying that there were no computers in heaven. *Where will that leave me when I get to heaven?* I thought. *Hopefully I'll find a golf course with long, straight fairways, but what would I do with my time away from the game without computers? How would God like for me to spend my eternity in paradise?*

I then remembered that the Bible often describes heaven as a joyous place filled with music and singing.

Perfect! I thought. *Through music, I can start preparing for heaven by studying a new activity that would be pleasing to God—and that I would enjoy!*

Thus, I went out and bought a guitar and began learning to play and sing our church music and spiritual songs. And so now, even though I'm no Ottmar Liebert or Chet Atkins, I truly enjoy strumming the strings in worship. I like reminding Christians, particularly the men, that it might be a good idea to get a head start on heaven by playing in the church band or singing in church every chance possible. How else are they going to learn the songs and music of worship before they arrive?

The *Catechism of the Catholic Church* defines purgatory as a "purification, so as to achieve the holiness necessary to enter the joy of heaven" (CCC 1031). However, you do not have to wait; it can start now. Jesus reassures us in John 5:24 that eternal life begins once a person follows His teachings and professes faith in the Father:

> Amen, amen, I say to you, whoever hears my word and believes in the one who sent me has eternal life and will not come to condemnation, but has passed from death to life.

Thus, your transformation can begin by simply letting the Holy Spirit into your heart and asking the Lord to help you. Ask to be changed:

- From selfishly getting your way to selflessly laying down your life.
- From asking, "What is in it for me?" to "Lord, what should I be doing with these gifts that have been put in my life?"
- From living in the flesh to living in the Spirit.

Make this change of heart and mind and you will see the benefits of love all around you.

It took the first several years of my marriage, and much shared anxiety and frustration, before I eventually figured this out. I find it hilariously ironic that in learning to show my wife and children how much I loved them, I needed to learn the value of showing my love to all.

Early in my marriage, I tried to selectively pick and choose to whom I was going to show love and caring. Living in the flesh, I thought that I could decide who was worthy of my love, and in my judgment I had decided that it would only be my wife and two sons. Others were excluded from my world of love. This was not a love in the Spirit. Jesus instructs in Matthew 5:44–45:

> But I say to you, love your enemies, and pray for those who persecute you, that you may be children of your heavenly Father, for he makes his sun rise on the bad and the good, and causes rain to fall on the just and the unjust.

If someone would have told me in the early years of my marriage that I should love my enemies, I would have said, "Hey, I'm not even sure I love my friends!"

My selectivity ultimately caused those three people whom I had chosen to love to actually believe that I did not love them at all. My family saw that I was living in the flesh, not living the fruit of the Spirit and not open to transformation.

Many of us unwittingly fall into this trap. Instead of loving as Christ taught us to love, our tendency is to only respond when others treat us well as a reward. That is judgment. "You do this for me, and I'll do this for you or reward you with my love." The lesson that I eventually learned, after almost driving away my family by trying to define my own way of loving, was that love must be 100 percent. It cannot be selective, and it cannot be redefined.

Once you allow the Holy Spirit to transform and guide you, your relationship with your spouse, as well as your other relationships, will begin to change. In any relationship, it only takes one person to be guided by the Holy Spirit to begin that transformation process. The other person will naturally respond, in some way. When Elaine and I made the decision to accept the Holy Spirit into our lives and put Christ at the center of our marriage, it started a chain reaction that changed not only our household but our entire circle of relationships.

THE SPIRITUAL STEPS TO A GREAT MARRIAGE

Throughout this book I have attempted to share my thoughts on many key strategies and elements of successful Christian marriages. These teachings and knowledge have been revealed to me and my wife through our life together and through our experiences of working together with couples who were intent on improving or saving their own marriages. Rather than write a feel-good book, my intent has been to give it to you straight; the objective has been to share practical solutions and guidance based on a deep understanding of committed, spiritually-based relationships and scriptural principles. This is a spiritual book, one that asks you to be willing to have the kind of relationship with your spouse that God has taught. As *The Spiritual Steps to a Great Marriage,* the following is a summary of several of the most valuable and meaningful concepts we've covered thus far:

1. *Prioritize God first, your spouse second,* and then all of your other relationships with family, friends, and coworkers. How is this done? It means focusing your mind on continually developing these relationships and allotting the proper amount of time and energy to those that matter most.

2. *Learn to manage conflicts and disagreements* in ways that will create opportunities to strengthen your relationships. Just as in a Christ-centered marriage, relationships that are built upon spiritual principles

can withstand any of life's messy situations or complicated dramas, and, in fact, can become sources of discovery and growth. When points of contention do arise, address the issues quickly and begin working toward a compromise. Also, take responsibility for your own negative emotions and manage your responses to life's challenges by following Christ's model for living. Your relationship's health means more than competing over who is right.

3. *Depend on Jesus to be the foundation* of your marriage and your personal development. As you draft the blueprint for your Christian marriage, allow His teachings and the model of His life to inspire your plan and decision-making. With Christ at the center of your lives and marriage, define what your relationship expectations and your shared and individual priorities are, as well as what you would like your ideal home life to be like. Look and live facing forward, and do not dwell upon the past.

4. *Share Christ in your marriage and with those around you* to whom you feel led to witness. As you accept Jesus' teachings and the Word of the LORD into your life, reveal how the Holy Spirit is working in you and the impact it is having in your heart and in your relationship with others.

5. *Live your Christian marriage daily* by doing those things that demonstrate your commitment to the relationship and to each other's happiness. Some of the key actions characteristic of great Christian marriages and relationships are open expressions of

love, laughter, having patience, sharing, playing, and praying together.

6. *Create an environment for open communications* that is both noncritical and nonjudgmental. Using the lessons from the Scripture as the model for good communications will help to bridge the gap between initial differences in communication styles. Oftentimes people simply need to feel as though they are being heard and their perspective is understood. Learning how to constructively listen will go a long way when communicating through difficult subjects or issues.

7. *Be willing to change* in order to improve your marriage, as there are no quick fixes. You must be willing to take responsibility for this transformation and let go of old self-centered habits and behaviors, no matter how out of your "comfort zone" they are. Focus on what you can do to make things better and not on criticizing or changing others. As your spiritual partner, give your spouse the right to help and correct you. Also, try setting an annual goal for yourself to change one to three things about yourself that will help you become more like Christ. Four of the major causes of marriage breakup are addictions and distractions, judgmentalism, unwillingness to change, and a loss of faith in marriage. Although these are characteristic of poor communications in many marriages, simply striving to be better than just half the marriages out there is not good enough.

8. *Be willing to forgive others* who may have upset or disappointed you. Forgive your persecutors, and look

for ways to create win-win situations. Just as importantly, remember to forgive God when the events in life do not seem to go the way in which you would like. His plan for you goes beyond your comprehension. And ultimately, forgive yourself when you make mistakes, as you are a child of God. Once we learn to forgive all, we are freed from the chains of past disappointments, and God will take us further. As Matthew 6:14–15 tells us:

> If you forgive others their transgressions, your heavenly Father will forgive you. But if you do not forgive others, neither will your Father forgive your transgressions.

Forgiveness is critical to becoming a more loving, Christ-like person doing the will of God.

9. *Take assessment of how satisfied you are in the key priorities in your life,* such as Family, Intellect, Social, Health, and Spiritual. Rate your level of satisfaction in each area from one to ten. What would it mean to score a one or a ten? If there are areas that you currently score poorly, what would you do differently to improve the score? Use this exercise to gain perspective on your top priorities and then to develop a balanced, integrated plan for how you intend to improve in those areas.

10. *Value each other's differences and abilities, working together* to overcome obstacles and pursuing shared goals. Rarely are spouses 100 percent alike in their

perspectives on money, decision-making, raising children, approaches to intimacy, communication, etc. By recognizing and appreciating your differences, you and spouse can become a team that is better equipped for success than a team without varied perspectives. As you work together, be sure to set realistic expectations and offer sincere appreciation for the effort that each contributes. When you respect and value your spouse's differences, you further prove that you are open to change.

11. *Have a servant spirit,* as we are all serving one another in unity and love in the kingdom of God here on earth. In all you do, do with passion and love, always striving to give your best and doing it better than what is expected. Pray for the wisdom that comes from a serving spirit and humility. As Jesus told us in Matthew 20:26–28:

> But it shall not be so among you. Rather, whoever wishes to be great among you shall be your servant; whoever wishes to be first among you shall be your slave. Just so, the Son of Man did not come to be served but to serve and to give his life as a ransom for many.

12. *Begin sharing the fruit of the Spirit* with others by allowing Christ to live at the center of your life and letting the power of the Holy Spirit transform you, guiding your thoughts and actions. Through your transformation you will become more Christ-like, sharing with others the fruit of the Holy Spirit,

which is love, joy, peace, patience, kindness, generosity, faithfulness, gentleness, and self-control. This will profoundly impact all of your personal and professional relationships.

13. *Cherish the sacrament of marriage,* as it is a covenant and not a contract. It signifies the developing and growing commitment between two people to act in love and loyalty to each other, no matter their circumstances or the consequences. This is quite different from marriage being simply a contractual agreement.

14. *Work to become a source of joy* in the lives of your spouse and family by putting the need to increase their happiness before your own. Families and spouses that continually participate together in positive, fun, stimulating, and interesting activities will strengthen and grow their relationships, as well as develop a foundation of love and trust that can be shared with the rest of the world. To paraphrase Mother Theresa of Calcutta, first spread love to your spouse and family, next to your friends and neighbors, and then everywhere you go. Let everyone who may come to you leave better and happier.

15. *Cherish your relationships* as you would a gift from God. Although your spouse has been personally anointed to help you transform, in each of the people who come and go in your life, there is the potential to hear God's voice. As He speaks to you through the words and actions of His children, use your best judgment to discern the lesson being shared. Because

each person is a messenger, try to understand their role in your life, and always share with them your love and respect.

UNCONDITIONAL LOVE AS SPIRITUAL INSPIRATION

Learning to love and respect your spouse is the key to developing a deeper spiritual relationship with God. The Apostle Paul compared the love that Jesus felt for the broader church to the love a man should feel for his wife, as described in Ephesians 5:25–30:

> Husbands, love your wives, even as Christ loved the church and handed himself over for her to sanctify her, cleansing her by the bath of water with the word, that he might present to himself the church in splendor, without spot or wrinkle or any such thing, that she might be holy and without blemish. So (also) husbands should love their wives as their own bodies. He who loves his wife loves himself. For no one hates his own flesh but rather nourishes and cherishes it, even as Christ does the church, because we are members of his body.

In this letter, Paul insists that a husband should love, cherish, and nourish his relationship with his wife. Serving as a model for both husbands and wives, it describes the spiritual purity of treating one's spouse with love and respect. God has called all of us to treat our spouses in that manner.

Paul then goes on to explain the mystery of the reference to Christ and the church in Ephesians 5:31: "For this reason a man shall leave (his) father and (his) mother and shall be joined to his wife, and the two shall become one flesh."

In 1 Peter 3:7–9, the message of showing respect to those who share our lives is echoed:

> Likewise, you husbands should live with your wives in understanding, showing honor to the weaker female sex, since we are joint heirs of the gift of life, so that your prayers may not be hindered. Finally, all of you, be of one mind, sympathetic, loving toward one another, compassionate, humble. Do not return evil for evil, or insult for insult; but, on the contrary, a blessing, because to this you were called, that you might inherit a blessing.

Essentially, unless we show consideration and caring, selfless love to our spouses, as well as any "fellow heir of the grace of life," we have no business asking God to honor our prayers. By this measure, making the decision to treat others poorly becomes a hindrance to God working in our lives. This is clearly spelled out in 1 John 4:20–21:

> If anyone says, "I love God," but hates his brother, he is a liar; for whoever does not love a brother whom he has seen cannot love God whom he has not seen. This is the commandment we have from him: whoever loves God must also love his brother.

Once we've made the decision to treat everyone, especially our spouses, with honor and respect, nothing will impede our prayers and prayer lives. But why is this so important? Our spouses and our children are gifts from God. If we do not fully love our gifts from God, then we are not letting the Holy Spirit transform us into our true loving potential. Our extended families, friends, and coworkers are also gifts. Learning how to love our gifts is the first test of all our relationships. Jesus tells us in Luke 12:25–26 that:

> Can any of you by worrying add a moment to your lifespan? If even the smallest things are beyond your control, why are you anxious about the rest?

In order for God to use us in larger ways, we must demonstrate that we have been fully transformed into loving beings. How we treat our families is a key indicator of readiness for:

- How we will be disciples of God
- How we are going to pursue God's calling for our lives
- How we will use the tools and talents He has given us
- How prepared we are for new challenges and opportunities
- How we can affect others and how our relationships will grow and evolve

Our calling to be transformed into loving, Christ-like people is the core truth that God has given us. Once again, as Jesus has told us in John 8:31–32:

> "If you remain in my word, you will truly be my disciples, and you will know the truth, and the truth will set you free."

As our model for this unconditional and limitless love, God gave us His Son, the earthly embodiment of selflessness, sacrifice, and complete giving. John 3:16–17 clearly proclaims that:

> For God so loved the world that he gave his only Son, so that everyone who believes in him might not perish but might have eternal life. For God did not send his Son into the world to condemn the world, but that the world might be saved through him.

Forty-seven years of marriage, children, grandchildren, ministry, friendships, successes, and mistakes, lean times and stout times, and helping others have taught my wife and me this truth: *Though we are all imperfect beings, with God's help, each of us is capable of loving unconditionally.* In your own marriage, and in all your relationships, great love is possible through the model of Christ's sacrifice. As committed followers of Christ, you and your spouse have a unique opportunity to love each other without limit or condition. Remember, as John 15:12–13 states:

> This is my commandment, love one another as I love you. No one has greater love than this, to lay down one's life for one's friends.

Clearly, the secret that God wants us to uncover is that through our expressions and actions of love, we will find life's ultimate meaning and fulfillment. In 1 John 4:7–8, we are given the origin, source, and promise of all love:

> Beloved, let us love one another, because love is of God; everyone who loves is begotten by God and knows God. Whoever is without love does not know God, for God is love.

Having the kind of marriage and relationships that are centered upon the life and teachings of Christ will take you along an incredible journey. In becoming an adept traveler, you will learn to be aware of the needs of your spouse and family, you will be willing to change, and you will then be open to personal transformation. God has given you the gift of marriage to serve as your catalyst for personal renewal and to fulfill the promise of selfless, unconditional love. The journey takes a lifetime lived one day at a time, yet the experiences you'll face will fill you with wisdom, peace, love, joy and many other spiritual fruit. *As you and your spouse voyage through life's adventures together, may the* L*ord* *be with you to become one with the help of the Holy Spirit.* As Paul offers in his letter to the Ephesians 3:14–21:

> For this reason I kneel before the Father, from whom every family in heaven and on earth is named, that he may grant you in accord with the riches of his glory to be strengthened with power through his Spirit in the inner self, and that Christ may dwell in your hearts through faith; that you, rooted and grounded

in love, may have strength to comprehend with all the holy ones what is the breadth and length and height and depth, and to know the love of Christ that surpasses knowledge, so that you may be filled with all the fullness of God. Now to him who is able to accomplish far more than all we ask or imagine, by the power at work within us, to him be glory in the church and in Christ Jesus to all generations, forever and ever. Amen.